Uniforms & Equipment of the Italian Armed Forces in World War I

Uniforms & Equipment of the Italian Armed Forces in World War I

Spencer A. Coil

Schiffer Military History
Atglen, PA

ACKNOWLEDGMENTS

First, and foremost, I would like to acknowledge and dedicate this work to all those who served in the Great War, especially those who appear in these photographs, and above all to my family, who supported and stood by me every step of the way, especially my ***Mother***, ***Aunt Frankie***, and ***Grandmother***!

I would like to thank the following individuals who directly or indirectly assisted in the creation of this work:

SUPERFOTO Studio, Marzio Bondavalli (professional photographer)
Professor Dr. Renato Zavattini and family (experts, specialists, enthusiasts, historians, authors)
Dr. Tazio Trivini Bellini (expert, specialist, enthusiast, historian)
Cesare Ceni (enthusiast, expert, specialist, historian, collector)
Marco Comini (enthusiast, expert, specialist, historian, collector)
Enzo Bajocchi (expert, specialist, enthusiast, historian)
Frédéric Gouraud (expert, specialist, enthusiast, historian)
Steve Smith Studios (professional photographers)
Salvatore Vasta, uniform specialist, founder, and curator of the Italian Front Group.
The Pomeranzeva-Halikin Family (historians, experts, enthusiasts, linguists)
The Hornkohl Family (enthusiasts)
The Otte Family (enthusiasts)
Alexei Grichine (expert, specialist, and enthusiast)
Frau Dr. Grafin Irene Montjoye and her son, Herr Mag. Graf Douglas Montjoye (authors, journalists, enthusiasts, historians)
Dan Eibeck (historian, expert, specialist, enthusiast, archaeologist)
Mag. Clemens Ellmauthaler (author, historian, expert, specialist, enthusiast)
Fulvio Rizzo (historian, expert, specialist, enthusiast)
Professor Del Schwinke
President Dr. David Harpool
President Dr. Wil Goodheer
Vice President Dr. L. Boyer
My Students

Many of the original period pieces featured in the color gallery are from the internationally acclaimed collection of Dr. Tazio Trivini Bellini.

A special thanks to internationally acclaimed and recognized military medals and decorations experts, specialists, and enthusiasts Herr und Frau Mag. Hartmut und Christine Rochowanski, who have maintained an impeccable reputation for over thirty years, and Franz Zabernig and family.

Finally, a very special thanks to the Schiffer team! They are all great to work with, and the books just keep getting better!

Book design by Ian Robertson.

Library of Congress Control Number: 2006927487

Printed in China.
ISBN: 0-7643-2536-1

We are interested in hearing from authors with book ideas on related topics.

Published by Schiffer Publishing Ltd.
4880 Lower Valley Road
Atglen, PA 19310
Phone: (610) 593-1777
FAX: (610) 593-2002
E-mail: Info@schifferbooks.com.
Visit our web site at: www.schifferbooks.com
Please write for a free catalog.
This book may be purchased from the publisher.
Please include $3.95 postage.
Try your bookstore first.

In Europe, Schiffer books are distributed by:
Bushwood Books
6 Marksbury Avenue
Kew Gardens
Surrey TW9 4JF, England
Phone: 44 (0) 20 8392-8585
FAX: 44 (0) 20 8392-9876
E-mail: Info@bushwoodbooks.co.uk.
Visit our website at: www.bushwoodbooks.co.uk
Free postage in the UK. Europe: air mail at cost.
Try your bookstore first.

Contents

Introduction

by Professor Dr. Renato Zavattini

"Tutti avevano la faccia del Cristo, nella livida aureola dell'elmetto,
tutti portavano l'insegna del supplizio nella croce della baionetta,
e nelle tasche il pane dell'Ultima Cena,
e nella gola il pianto dell'ultimo Addio"
(Anonimo, galleria delle Tofane)

"All of them had the face of Christ, in the livid aureole of the helmet,
all of them bear the standard of the torment in the cross of the bayonet,
and in their pockets the bread of the Last Supper,
and in the throat the cry of the last Farewell"
(Anonymous, in a gallery located in the Tofane mountain range)

Before the appearance of the Model 1909 *grigioverde* (grey green) uniform, the Italian armed forces were diverse in their outfitting, and experimented with various models of uniforms. Diversity in outfitting was due in part to the wars for the unification of Italy fought in the previous century, as well as how industry was organized in the country. Pre to early war uniforms were predominantly dark blue in color; however, the armed forces also experimented with other colors and styles. An example of an experimental model which was employed before the Model 1909 *grigioverde* (grey green) uniform can be seen in the formation of the "grey platoon." The "grey platoon" was a platoon of *Alpini* (Alpine troops) outfitted with grey uniforms during the beginning of the twentieth century. This signalled the gradual end of the use of the color dark blue, which later was used for parades and other occasions. Henceforth, when a soldier entered the armed forces as of 1909 he was said to be in the "*grigioverde*," or the official color of uniforms, whether it was depot issued or privately purchased.

Headdresses

A *berretto* (field cap) was worn by *Fanteria* (Infantry) as well as other units, and either was depot issued or privately purchased. The Model 1909 *berretto* varied in shape and size, but could easily be distinguished from the Model 1915, often referred to as a *cupolino* (little dome) or *scodellino* (little bowl). The main differences between the two models were in the shapes and materials used. The Model 1909 was cylindrical in shape, and was fashioned from various types of material, while the Model 1915 was more dome shaped, and was mainly made of pressed and starched felt. A similar evolution in field caps can be seen in the Austro-Hungarian armed forces as well. The Austro-Hungarian *Feldkappe* (field cap), which was depot issued or privately purchased, had a teardrop or cylindrical shape, and was often replaced by a privately purchased dome shaped field cap (See *Uniforms and Equipment of the Austro-Hungarian Army page 331*). The culture of wearing *Kappeabzeichen* (cap badges) on *berretti* was not followed very often as it was in the Austro-Hungarian armed forces. Unit and rank insignia always appeared on *berretti* unless removed, covered, or subdued for camouflage purposes.

In addition to the Model 1909, a soldier could also wear a cloth *berretto a due punte* (two pointed forage/tent cap without a visor), or a *cappello a visera a due punte* (two-pointed forage/tent cap with a visor). This headdress could also be either depot issued or privately purchased. In addition, there is a misspelling in the headdress section about the *besaglieri*. The correct spelling for the plumes is *piumetto*.

Alpini (Alpine troops) headdress remained the traditional *cappello* and was made of rabbit fur felt and varied in shape and size. An *Alpino* could privately purchase his *cappello* as well as obtaining one from a supply depot. *Penne nere* or black feathers were often worn by *Alpini* and were placed in a holder known as *nappina*. The color of *nappina* also determined an *Alpino's* battalion or unit. For example, a white *nappina* was for first battalion, red for second battalion, green for third battalion, blue for fourth battalion and yellow for general staff and depot units. Unit and rank insignia was also fastened on an *Alpino's cappello.*

Bersaglieri (Elite/Guard/Rifle troops) maintained the traditional *moretto* with *puimetto* (plumes) until they were issued Model 1915 Adrian helmets in 1916. The traditional *moretto* was dome shaped and had a wide round brim with a holder on the side for the *puimetto.* Unit insignia was normally made of brass and fastened to the front.

A *bersagliere* could also purchase his *moretto* privately or have one issued to him from a supply depot. In addition to the *moretto*, a *bersagliere* could also wear a madder red fez with tassel.

Carabinieri (Gendarme/Military Police) also maintained their traditional tricorn headdress known as a *lucerna*. This headdress was rarely, if ever, was worn on the frontlines. A *lucerna*, as with other headdresses, were issued with fitted cloth covers, which served as protection as well as camouflage purposes.

Cavalry headdresses, such as those worn by *dragoni* (dragoons) and *lancieri* (lancers), still reflected influence from the previous century. The *Model 1910 Dragone* as well as variations on the Models 1833 or 1842 were worn by dragoons upon Italy's initial entry into the War and were later abandoned for use on the frontlines and reserved for parades or other occasions. *Lancieri* wore a headdress known as a *colbacco*, which was cylindrically shaped and made of fur or felt.

The Farina and the Adrian helmets were the principle helmets of the Italian armed forces and were usually only issued to frontline combat units. The first Farina helmets were issued in *grigioverde* while the first Adrian helmets were issued in *bleu horizon* (horizon blue) and later painted *grigioverde*. Farina helmets proved to provide protection however were heavy and decreased a soldier's manoeuvrability. Adrian helmets were lighter weight and had unit insignia stencilled on the front of the helmet above the visor. A captured *Stahlhelm* (steel helmet) or an Austro-Hungarian manufactured Berndorfer was also occasionally worn as well.

As did other armed forces of the participating nations in the First World War, the Italian armed forces also wore headdresses such as, canvas covered cork pith helmets and leather or oilcloth covered helmets. Canvas covered cork pith helmets would have been worn in warmer climates such as, the Balkans or Libya while motorists, motorcyclists and aviators would have worn leather or oilcloth-covered helmets.

Tunics

One version of the Model 1909 tunic existed for infantry and other units while another version was made for cavalry units. The infantry and other units version had the so-called *salsicciotti* (sausages), which are rounded raised reinforcements on the shoulders of the tunic. The cavalry version had shoulder straps sewn on the outer edge of the shoulder held in place by buttons. Both the infantry *salsicciotti* and the cavalry style shoulder strap served the purpose of holding other straps or slings in place while horseback riding or during a rigorous march. Both versions when depot issued and sometimes privately tailored had five concealed buttons. Privately tailored tunics usually had exposed buttons and exterior pockets. These tunics were worn by NCOs or enlisted ranked *Soldati* (soldiers/troopers) who took the effort to have a tunic tailored privately. The collars on both versions had badges or patches identifying a Corp or Regiment. *Stellette* (metal stars) fastened to the collar with a pin, screw or brad on the reverse side. Specialty badges or patches were usually fastened or stitched to the left sleeve while rank distinctions were usually worn on the cuffs. Cavalry shoulder straps or infantry *salsicciotti* often had numbers or letters designating a unit.

With the formation of the elite assault units, such as the famed and legendary *Arditi* (bold/fearless ones) in 1917, yet another style of tunic was designed and issued. These tunics were worn with an open-collar and tailored from various materials. The collar badges or patches for this tunic were designed to look like black flames with two tips. *Stellette* were worn on the collar as well.

In addition, *grigioverde* colored waistcoats with five buttons and four chest and side pockets were often worn under the tunics.

Trousers

The trousers of units on foot with the exception of *Alpini* units were made of *grigoverde* colored material and had straps to tighten around the ankles. Two pockets were located on the sides and followed the seams. On the reverse side of the trousers was an adjustable strap with a black metal buckle and five buttons.

Trousers worn by *Alpini* were cut wider and shorter and ended at the calf where they were fastened with straps. From the knee going down to foot, the trousers were wrapped with *mollettiere* (puttees/leggings). Pre to early war photos show a baggier fitting trouser than those worn in the final days of the First World War.

Mounted units wore trousers wide in the thigh region and close fitting around the calf. These trousers were often reinforced on the inner side of the knees and fit usually high on the waistline. Trousers were occasionally lined depending upon the availability of material.

Outerwear

Foot soldiers were issued *grigioverde* colored heavy cloth single-breasted overcoats, which often had *stellette* on the collar. Mounted troops generally wore issued or privately tailored double-breasted four pocketed overcoats with concealed buttons. The collars were usually wider on these overcoats and the shoulder straps were removable as well. Fur and leather overcoats were also worn when available.

A short *mantellina* (cape/cloak) made from treated grey burlap was manufactured in the only one size and was issued from supply depots. However, many *Soldati* (soldiers/troopers) obtained privately tailored ones made of *grigioverde* wool. *Stellette* was often fastened to a *mantellina* if it had a collar.

Brown wool gloves were issued to all units except motorcyclists, drivers, *bersaglieri* cyclist and *bersaglieri*. These units were instead issued with black wool gloves. Most *Soldati* supplied their own gloves when they had the opportunity.

Footwear

The issued hobnails boots with laces were made of black or brown colored calfskin leather. *Alpini* units were issued leather boots with cleats on the soles and with reinforced tips and heels. Sentries wore boots with wooden soles instead of leather because of their exposure to the weather. Mounted units generally wore riding boots, which were pulled on using leather or canvas straps. Footwear could also be privately purchased as well.

As with all armies during the First World War, the Italian army had difficulties supplying footwear especially for the harsh conditions of the trenches. Two pair of boots issued to each *Soldato* (soldier) proved to be insufficient.

Equipment

In addition to their weaponry, *Soldati* were issued equipment and accessories. Many of the items were made domestically and others were imported from abroad. These issued items included a Model 1907 haversack, backpack, leather ammo pouches, Model 1891 belt with bayonet frog, Model 1897 bandolier, Model 1876, 1907, 1909, 1917 canteens, *polivalente* or other foreign manufactured gas masks and any other items available at the depot.

The Model 1907 haversack and backpack were made of treated grey burlap with burnished metal and *grigioverde* colored leather fittings. Various models of canteens such as the 1907, 1909, 1917 could be fastened inside or outside of the haversack or backpack.

Canteens varied in design and materials used in construction. The Model 1907 was wood with metal fittings and had a cloth-carrying strap. The Model 1876 was also made of the same material, however it had a leather carrying harness. The Models 1909 and 1917 had leather-carrying harnesses as well. The 1909 and 1917 were made of metal and had wool covers.

Leather items such as bayonet frogs, bandoliers, ammunition pouches, belts and straps were either colored *grigioverde* or left in a natural finish. When leather was not available to manufacture these items, other materials were substituted.

The aforementioned equipment items were normally domestically manufactured. The *polivalente* gasmask was domestically manufactured, but other gasmasks had to be imported from the United States, Britain and France. Captured gasmasks were also used as well.

Observations, Nuances, and Conclusions on the Italian Armed Forces

The Italian armed forces had to adapt and change just as the other nations had to fighting the Great War. Domestic industry was not readily capable of meeting the needs of these adaptations and changes the armed forces required. Therefore, the armed forces had to import items from other countries, use captured equipment and make innovative changes and adaptations to existing equipment and uniform designs.

Above all, the Italian armed forces did show the World it could suffer defeats and still make a comeback.

Chapter One

Machineguns

(Mitragliatrici)

This soldier (*soldato*) wearing a gray green (*grigioverde*) wool Model 1909 tunic and Model 1915 Adrian steel helmet poses proudly with his Model 1889 revolver in his right hand, and a Model 1914 Fiat-Revelli machinegun mounted on a tripod (*Mitragliatrice Fiat-Revelli Modello 1914*) on his right side. On the reverse of this photo another *soldato* writes in Italian how this machinegunner of the 748th Company, 2nd Section, was killed by his side on May 21, 1917. He goes on to write " I give this photo to the family of this brave man. This is the weapon he was using, and with the same weapon we will avenge him—fighting to the end!"

A mustached soldier wearing a gray green wool Model 1909 field cap and tunic pauses for a photo while seated on his 8mm Lebel caliber Model 1907 Saint Etienne machinegun (*Mitragliatrice Saint Etienne modello 1907 calibro 8mm Lebel*).

Four soldiers (*soldati*) armed with a 8mm Lebel caliber Model 1907 Saint Etienne machinegun (*Mitragliatrice Saint Etienne modello 1907 calibro 8mm Lebel*) and Model 1891 rifles pause for a photo in their trench. In addition, all four wear gray green (*grigioverde*) wool Model 1909 tunics and Model 1915 Adrian steel helmets.

Six soldiers wearing gray green (*grigioverde*) wool Model 1909 tunics and Model 1915 Adrian steel helmets pose proudly with their 8mm Lebel caliber Model 1907 Saint Etienne machinegun (*Mitragliatrice Saint Etienne modello 1907 calibro 8mm Lebel*).

A group of soldiers (*soldati*) wearing gray green Model 1909 field caps and tunics pose in a courtyard for a photo with their two 8mm Lebel caliber Model 1907 Saint Etienne machineguns. The soldier seated in front wearing a Red Cross armband on his left sleeve is a medic. He carries a medical pouch like the one featured in the *Color Gallery*.

In a field near the front, five soldiers wearing gray green (*grigioverde*) Model 1909 tunics and Model 1915 Adrian helmets pose proudly with their 8mm Lebel caliber Model 1907 Saint Etienne machinegun (*Mitragliatrice Saint Etienne modello 1907 calibro 8mm Lebel*).

A group of soldiers (*soldati*) wearing gray green (*grigioverde*) wool Model 1909 tunics and Model 1915 Adrian steel helmets line up with their 8mm Lebel caliber Model 1907 Saint Etienne machineguns in a field near the frontlines.

Officers, NCOs, and enlisted rank troops wearing gray green Model 1909 field caps and tunics pose for a photo armed with two Model 1911 Vickers Maxims, as well as an assortment of pistols and revolvers. The cloth number "31" stitched to their field caps indicates their unit.

In an encampment near the frontlines, eight soldiers pose for a photo outside their tent with their tripod mounted Model 1914 Fiat-Revelli machineguns.

This mustached soldier poses for a photo in the field wearing a Model 1909 tunic made of gray green wool with a decoration bar stitched to it. The cloth insignia stitched to his left sleeve indicates he is in a machinegun unit.

The 2nd Lieutenant (*Sottotenente*) seated in this photo wears a privately tailored double breast pocketed gray green (*grigioverde*) wool tunic (*Giacca*) with a decoration bar stitched above his left breast pocket. He has machinegun unit insignia stitched to both sleeves of his tunic.

Machinegunners pose proudly for a 1916 vintage group photo. Note the officer dressed in a black uniform. The black uniform was permissable to wear during the First World War, however, not on the frontlines.

Chapter Two

Medical

(Sanita)

En route to the frontlines, an American ambulance driver stops to change a tire while his Italian comrades watch.

These four medics are clad in gray green (*grigioverde*) wool Model 1909 tunics, 1917.

The mustached medic holding his overcoat in this 1916 vintage studio photo wears a *grigioverde*, or gray green wool Model 1909 field tunic and cap. In addition, he has cloth rank insignia stitched on both cuffs of his tunic, as well as two metal five pointed stars (*Stellette*) fastened to his collar.

This mustached medic wears a Model 1912 gray cotton uniform based on the Model 1909. His Model 1909 field cap appears to be made of wool, with a leather chinstrap and visor. 1915/1916.

With his right arm resting upon an intricately carved pedestal, a mustached medic poses proudly in this 1917 vintage studio photo wearing a Model 1909 field cap and tunic made of *grigioverde*, or gray green wool. In addition, he is armed with a Vetterli bayonet, which hangs on his left side.

The medic in this studio photo wears a tunic, pair of pants, and gaiters made of *grigioverde* (gray green wool). He has placed his Model 1909 field cap bearing cloth medical unit insignia on the chair beside him.

The mustached medic seated in this studio photo wears an issue Model 1909 tunic made of gray green wool with a Red Cross brassard on his left sleeve. The raised wool pads on the shoulders of his tunic helped to hold a rifle sling in place.

Nurses, surgeons, and patients pose for a photo in a hospital near the front, 1917.

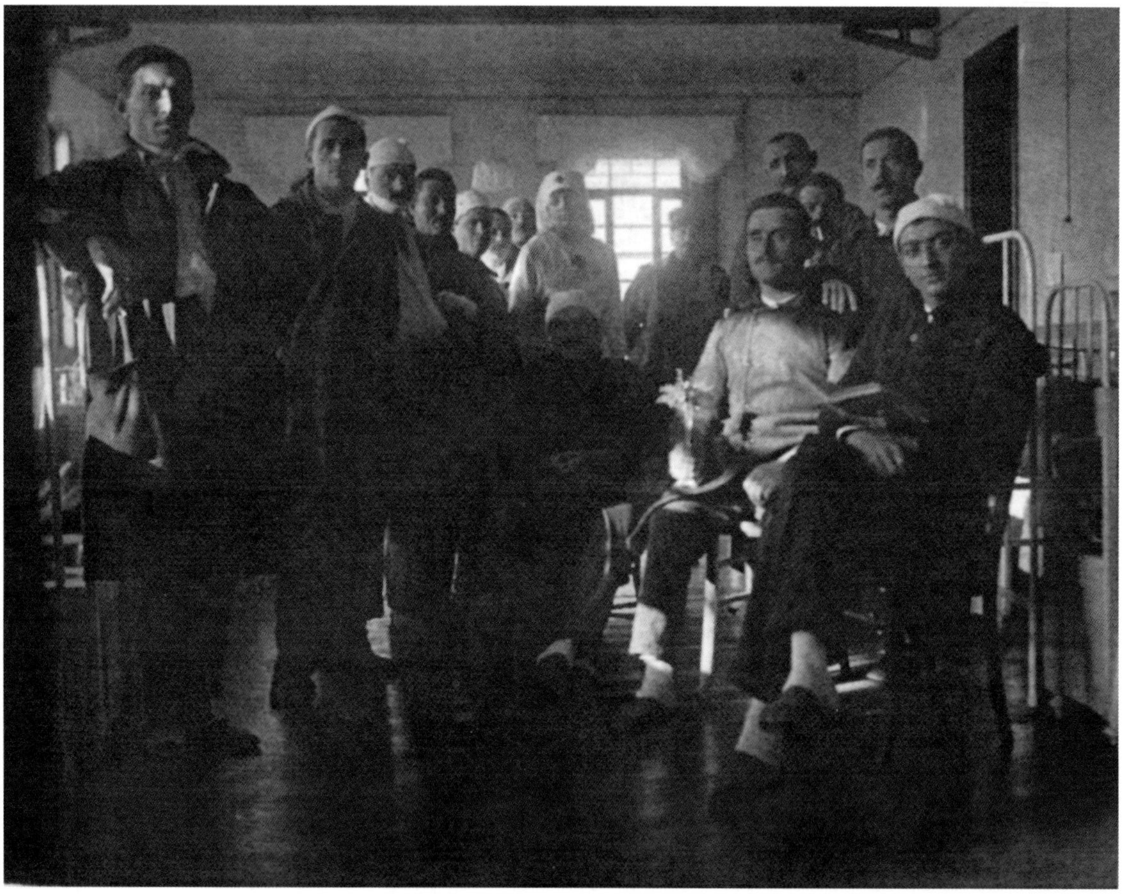

A nurse poses for a photo with her patients at a hospital near the frontlines.

The mustached medic in this 1917 vintage studio photo wears a *grigioverde*, or gray green wool Model 1909 tunic with metal five pointed star (*Stellette*) insignia fasted to his collar, and a cloth Red Cross brassard on his left sleeve.

The mustached medic resting his arm on the pedestal in this 1917 vintage studio photo wears a Model 1909 tunic and field cap. In addition, he has cloth medical unit insignia stitched to his field cap, and two metal five-pointed stars fastened to the collar of his tunic.

Two medics and a military chaplain with a black cross stitched to his tunic pose for a photo with their canine companion.

Chapter Three

General Infantry

(Fanteria)

The mustached soldier (*soldato*) with the rank of *sergente maggiore* in this 1917 vintage photo poses proudly wearing a gray green wool (*grigioverde*) Model 1909 tunic (*Giacca*) with cloth rank chevrons stitched to his sleeves, and two five point metal star insignia fastened to his collar. The raised pads on the end of shoulders keep his rifle from slipping. In addition, he wears a leather Model 1907 equipment belt with ammo pouches (*Giberna*) that hold 6.5 mm caliber rounds.

The young soldier in this studio photo wears an issued tunic (*Giacca*) and cap (*Berretto*) made of gray green (*grigioverde*) wool. The number 91 stitched to his cap indicates his unit.

The mustached soldier (*soldato*) in this studio photo wears a gray green wool Model 1909 tunic with metal five-point star insignia fastened to his collar. His Model 1909 field cap with the number 8 stitched above the visor rests atop his gray green wool overcoat with cloth five point star (*Stellette*) insignia stitched to the collar, which he has draped over a pedestal. His left hand grips a Vetterli bayonet.

The three mustached NCOs in this 1916 vintage photo pose proudly wearing gray green (*grigioverde*) wool Model 1909 tunics with cloth rank chevrons stitched to their sleeves, and two five point metal star (*Stellette*) insignia fastened to their collars. Stitched on their Model 1909 field caps (*Berretti*) is the number 72, which indicates their unit.

With his right hand resting on a pedestal, this soldier (*soldato*) poses for a studio photo wearing a light colored cotton tunic and trousers. Cotton was often preferred, because it was easier to maintenance. Such uniforms usually were boiled in hot water as well to prevent diseases. His Model 1909 field cap, bearing the number 86, is made of wool with a leather visor and chip strap.

The mustached soldier in this studio photo wears a gray green (*grigioverde*) wool Model 1909 tunic (*Giacca*) and field cap. In addition, he has his gray green wool overcoat tucked under his right arm, and wears a dark colored brassard on the left sleeve of his tunic.

With his arm resting on a pedestal, this soldier (*soldato*) poses proudly in this 1917 vintage studio photo wearing a gray green wool field tunic and cap. The 83 stitched to his field cap indicates his unit. He appears to be armed with an Austro-Hungarian manufactured M95 bayonet.

The 2nd Lieutenant (*Sottotenente*) in this studio photo wears a privately tailored, double breast pocketed gray green (*grigioverde*) wool tunic (*Giacca*) based on the Model 1909. The number 22 in the center of his cap insignia indicates his unit.

The officer in this photo wears a privately tailored double breast pocketed gray green tunic and field cap based on the Model 1909, and fashioned from a coarse grade of wool. The number 15 fastened to the cloth insignia above the leather chinstrap and visor indicates his unit.

This soldier (*soldato*) wears a privately tailored gray green (*grigioverde*) wool tunic (*Giacca*) fashioned after the Model 1909. His unit number appears to be 17.

The mustached soldier with the rank of *sergente* seated in this 1917 vintage photo wears a Model 1909 field cap and tunic made of gray green wool. He has rank chevrons stitched to the sleeves of his tunic, and his unit number 26 stitched to his field cap.

Seated in this studio photo is a mustached enlisted rank (*Fante*) soldier wearing an issued gray green (*grigioverde*) Model 1909 tunic (*Giacca*), trousers, and puttees. He has a turtleneck sweater rolled over the collar of his tunic to protect his neck from rubbing against it.

This bearded captain (*Capitano*) in this studio photo wears a privately tailored gray green (*grigioverde*) wool field tunic (*Giacca*) and cap (*Berretto*) fashioned after the Model 1909. His unit insignia is stitched across the rank stripes on his field cap, and he has decoration ribbons stitched to his tunic.

The lieutenant (*Tenente*) seated in this studio photo wears a privately tailored double breast pocketed gray green (*grigioverde*) wool field tunic (*Giacca*) and cap (*Berretto*). His unit insignia is stitched across the rank stripes on his field cap.

This soldier wears a privately tailored double breast pocketed gray green field tunic (*Giacca*) based on the Model 1909, and made from a coarse grade of wool. His Model 1909 field cap (*Berretto*) is made from the same grade of wool, and has cloth unit insignia stitched above the leather chinstrap and visor. The number 81 indicates his unit.

The soldier (*soldato*) in this studio photo wears a privately tailored double breast pocketed tunic made of gray green (*grigioverde*) wool. He has a turtleneck sweater rolled over the collar of his tunic to protect his neck from rubbing against the wool of his tunic. His Model 1909 field cap has cloth infantry unit insignia and bears the number 50, indicating his unit. The lanyard around his neck attaches to his sidearm.

This mustached officer wears a gray green wool field tunic (*Giacca*) and cap (*Berretto*) fashioned after the Model 1909. He is armed with a Model 1888 saber (*Sciabola*).

With his hand resting near a vase of flowers, this young soldier (*soldato*) poses proudly in his issue gray green wool field tunic and cap. He has five pointed metal star (*Stellette*) insignia fastened to the collar of his tunic, and cloth unit insignia stitched above the leather visor and chinstrap of his cap. His puttees (*Mollettiere*), trousers (*Pantaloni*), and ankle boots (*Scarpe*) appear to be issue, as well.

This mustached soldier wears a privately tailored double breast pocketed tunic (*Giacca*) made of gray green (*grigioverde*) wool fashioned after the Model 1909, with a silk decoration ribbon (*Nastrino*) stitched above his left breast pocket. He grips a Model 1907 saber (*Sciabola*) with his left hand.

With two medals fastened to his issue gray green wool tunic, this mustached soldier poses proudly for a 1917 vintage studio photo. In addition, he wears an issue Model 1909 field cap with the number 122, and crown made of cloth stitched above the leather visor and chinstrap.

The soldier in this studio wears a gray green (*grigioverde*) wool cloak (*Mantellina*), tunic (*Giacca*), and cap (*Berretto*). The insignia stitched on the collar of his *Giacca* and *Mantellina*, as well as on his *Berretto*, indicates he is in the 2nd Grenadiers (*Granatieri*) Regiment.

These infantrymen pause for a photo clad in gray green (*grigioverde*) wool field tunics and caps. The officer on the right, wearing a cloak, rests his hand on his Model 1888 saber.

In this late war vintage studio photo, four infantrymen pose proudly wearing privately made gray green (*grigioverde*) wool tunics and caps based on the Model 1909.

The soldier (*soldato*) in studio photo wears a privately tailored, double breast pocketed gray green wool tunic (*Giacca*) fashioned after the Model 1909. The stitched insignia on his sleeve indicates that he is in a technical unit.

With his saber under his arm and his hand clenching his gloves, this soldier poses for a late war vintage studio photo wearing a privately tailored gray green wool tunic and field cap. In addition, he wears a leather ammo bandolier across his chest.

The soldier from a fortress artillery unit in this studio photo wears a pre to early war dark colored wool field cap and gray green wool overcoat.

The mustached solider (*soldato*) seated in this studio photo wears a privately tailored, doubled breast pocketed gray green wool tunic styled after the Model 1909, with five pointed star (*Stellette*) insignia fastened to his collar and shoulder boards (*Spalline*). In addition, he holds his privately made field cap in his left hand, and his Model 1888 saber and gloves in his right.

In a wooded area near the front lines, this mustached soldier pauses for a photo wearing an issue gray green (*grigioverde*) wool field cap (*Berretto*) and tunic (*Giacca*), as well as a pair of pants and puttees.

With his arm resting on an intricately carved banister, this mustached soldier poses proudly wearing issue gray green wool trousers and puttees. His field tunic and cap are made of gray green wool, and appear to be issue as well.

The soldier (*soldato*) in this late war vintage studio photo wears a gray green (*grigioverde*) wool tunic (*Giacca*) based on the cut of the Model 1909. He has a decoration ribbon (*Nastrino*) stitched to his chest, as well.

The dark haired and mustached soldier seated in this studio photo wears a gray green (*grigioverde*) wool tunic (*Giacca*) fashioned after the Model 1909. In addition, he has metal five pointed star (*Stellette*) insignia fastened to his collar, and cloth unit numbers stitched to his shoulder straps (*Spalline*).

The soldier (*soldato*) seated in this studio photo wears a privately tailored double breast pocketed gray green (*grigioverde*) wool tunic (*Giacca*) based on the Model 1909, with two five pointed metal star (*Stellette*) insignia fastened to his collar.

This soldier (*soldato*) wears a privately tailored double breast pocketed gray green wool field tunic (*Giacca*) fashioned after the Model 1909, with two five-pointed metal star (*Stellette*) insignia fastened to the collar. His Model 1909 field cap (*Berretto*) is made of gray green wool with a leather chinstrap and visor, and appears to be issue without unit insignia.

With his right hand holding his leather ammo bandolier, this bearded soldier poses for a photo wearing a gray green (*grigioverde*) wool Model 1909 field tunic and cap. His rank chevrons are stitched to the cuffs of his tunic.

Holding his saber (*Sciabola*) under his left arm, the soldier (*soldato*) in this late war vintage photo poses proudly wearing a privately tailored double breast pocketed gray green (*grigioverde*) wool tunic (*Giacca*) based on the Model 1909, with two five pointed metal stars (*Stellette*) insignia fastened to the collar.

The soldier seated in this studio photo wears a gray green wool Model 1909 tunic and leather gloves. His field boots (*Scarpe*) appear to be privately purchased, and not issued from a supply depot.

This soldier (*soldato*) wears a gray green (*grigioverde*) wool tunic (*Giacca*) with rank chevrons stitched to the sleeves, and five pointed metal star (*Stellette*) insignia fastened to his collar. The spurs (*Speroni*) on his boots (*Stivali*) indicate he is in a mounted unit.

These four *soldati* (soldiers) in this late war vintage studio photo confidently pose wearing their cotton tunics. Cotton was often preferred over wool because it was easier to maintain, and was boiled in water, making it more sanitary. Wearing the tunic with open collar, as three of these soldiers are doing, was a style preferred by the *Arditi*, who were the bold and fearless assault troops.

The soldier with his arms crossed in this studio photo wears a tunic (*Giacca*) made of gray green (*grigioverde*) wool. He has gold stitched rank chevrons stitched to his cuffs, and wears a high collar shirt to keep the collar of his *giacca* wool from rubbing against his neck.

The dark haired soldier (*soldato*) seated in this studio photo wears an issued tunic made from a coarse grade of gray green (*grigioverde*) wool. In addition, he has five-pointed metal star (*Stellette*) insignia fastened to his collar.

Four soldiers enjoying a drink pose proudly for a late war vintage studio photo wearing issued Model 1909 tunics made of gray green wool. The man wearing a suit with a tri-colored brassard on his left sleeve works in a factory engaged in wartime production.

The mustached soldier in this studio photo wears an issued gray green wool Model 1909 tunic with five-pointed metal star insignia fastened to the collar. He is armed with a Vetterli bayonet.

In this rustic looking studio photo, a mustached soldier (*soldato*) poses confidently wearing an issue Model 1909 tunic (*Giacca*) made of gray green (*grigioverde*) wool. His trousers, puttees (*Mollettiere*), and shoes (*Scarpe*) appear to be issued from a depot, as well.

Standing on a fur rug in a studio, this soldier poses for a photo wearing a gray green wool Model 1909 tunic with five pointed metal star collar insignia fastened to his collar. His right hand clutches a leather ammo bandolier.

In a wood near the front, a mustached soldier (*soldato*) poses for a photo wearing a double breast and side pocketed tunic (*Giacca*) that appears to have been manufactured from an ersatz material.

These three mustached enlisted rank soldiers pose confidently in this studio photo wearing issued gray green (*grigioverde*) wool Model 1909 tunics.

This dark haired soldier (*soldato*) wears an issued Model 1909 tunic (*Giacca*) made of gray green (*grigioverde*) wool with five pointed metal star (*Stellette*) insignia fastened to the collar.

The mustached solider with his hand on the chair in this studio photo wears a Model 1909 tunic made of gray green (*grigioverde*) wool. He wears gaiters instead of puttees. This photo was taken in Firenze, Italy.

These three dark haired soldiers wearing gray green wool tunics have their unit insignia (*automitragliatrici*) stitched to their sleeves. In addition, all three are equipped with leather ammo bandoliers.

The lieutenant (*Tenente*) seated with his arms folded in this late war vintage studio photo wears a privately tailored double breast pocketed gray green wool (*grigioverde*) tunic (*Giacca*) based on the Model 1909. He has decoration ribbons stitched above his left breast pocket.

This soldier wears a gray green (*grigioverde*) wool tunic (*Giacca*) with rank chevrons stitched to his sleeves, and five pointed metal star (*Stellette*) collar insignia fastened to his collar. This is a fascinating photo, because an infantry corporal (*Córporale*) is wearing a Model 1909 tunic for mounted troops.

The soldier poses proudly for a photo wearing a Model 1912 gray cotton uniform (*Uniforma da Fatica Mod.1912*). The propellor insignia on his cap indicates he is in an air service unit.

These four mustached *soldati* (soldiers) pose confidently in this late war vintage studio photo wearing gray green (*grigioverde*) wool tunics. This photo displays the various shades of *grigioverde* wool available for making a soldier's clothing.

This soldier poses proudly for a photo dressed in a cotton tunic and trousers. Uniforms made of cotton were preferred by many, particularly, those who served in Libya. The insignia on his gray green wool Model 1909 field cap indicates he is with the grenadiers, or *granatieri*.

With his left hand holding the back rest of a chair, this mustached soldier poses for a photo wearing a gray green (*grigioverde*) wool tunic (*Giacca*), and a cap (*Berretto*) resembling a French kepi.

Two soldiers (*soldati*) wearing gray green (*grigioverde*) wool tunics pose for a photo with a small child standing on a chair. The soldier on the left wears a field cap (*Berretto*) resembling a French kepi. The soldier on the right wears a *grigioverde* wool *berretto* fashioned after the Model 1909, which has a crushed look.

The mustached soldier, seated on a bench outside his barracks, wears a privately tailored double breast pocketed gray green wool tunic based on the Model 1909.

The soldier (*soldato*) in this shadowy studio photo wears a privately tailored double breast pocketed gray green (*grigioverde*) wool tunic styled after the Model 1909. This photo displays his unit insignia (*automitragliatrici*) on his sleeve.

This mustached soldier poses proudly in a rustic looking studio photo wearing a Model 1909 gray green wool tunic and field cap. He has a decoration ribbon (*Nastrino*) stitched to his tunic, and five point metal star (*Stellette*) insignia fastened to his collar. The insignia stitched on his field cap, as well as on his collar, indicates he is a grenadier, or *granatieri* regiment.

The young soldier in this studio photo wears an issued gray green (*grigioverde*) wool field tunic, cap, and trousers. His unit numbers are stitched above the leather visor of his field cap, and he has machinegunners insignia stitched to the sleeves of his tunic.

These two soldiers wear issued Model 1909 gray green wool tunics and trousers. Wearing heavy wool socks with the tops rolled down (right) was sometimes preferred to wool puttees (left).

The dark haired and mustached soldier (*soldato*) in this oval shaped studio photo wears an issued gray green (*grigioverde*) wool tunic with five pointed metal star (*Stellette*) insignia fastened to the collar.

This soldier wears an issued Model 1909 gray green wool tunic and trousers. He has rank chevrons stitched to his cuffs, and five pointed metal star insignia fastened to his collar. His Model 1909 gray green wool field cap appears to be privately purchased, and has a higher and stiffer shape than those normally issued. In addition, he has grenadiers (*granatieri*) insignia stitched above the leather chinstrap and visor of his field cap, and on the collar of his tunic.

The mustached soldier holding a pair of leather gloves in his left hand in this studio photo has the rank of *caporale maggiore* (roughly the equivalent of a corporal), as the rank stripes on the cuffs of his gray green wool tunic (*Giacca*) indicate. He has a crown and the number two stitched above the leather visor and chinstrap of his gray green wool Model 1909 field cap.

With his right hand behind his back, and his left hand holding a cigarette, this mustached soldier (*soldato*) poses confidently for a studio photo wearing an issued Model 1909 tunic and field cap made from a coarse grade of gray green wool. The crown and the number 12 stitched above the leather visor and chinstrap of his field cap, or *berretto*, indicate his unit. The 12th Infantry Regiment (*Brigata Casale*) fought bravely on the Isonzo Front, Podgoda, Monte Calvario, and in the Battle of Gorizia.

With his right hand resting on a pedestal next to his gray green wool Model 1909 field cap (*Berretto*), this soldier (*soldato*) poses proudly wearing an issued Model 1909 tunic (*Giacca*) made of gray green wool. In addition, he has a gray green wool cloak draped over his shoulders with five pointed star insignia on the collar.

The two soldiers in this studio photo wear field tunics and caps made of coarse gray green wool. The soldier on the left is a *caporale* (roughly the equivalent of a corporal), as the rank chevrons on the cuffs of his tunic (*Giacca*) indicate.

The dark haired officer wearing a privately tailored gray green (*grigioverde*) wool tunic (*Giacca*) with decoration ribbon (*Nastrino*) pauses from his desk work for this late war vintage photo.

The mustached soldier in this circular studio photo wears a Model 1909 gray green wool tunic and a Model 1915 field cap (*Scodellino*) made of gray green wool, as well. The number 68 stitched to his *scodellino* indicates his unit.

This soldier (*soldato*) wears a privately tailored double breast pocketed gray green (*grigio-verde*) wool tunic (*Giacca*) with brass buttons and five pointed star collar insignia.

With his right hand resting on a chair, the soldier in this studio photo wears an issued Model 1909 field cap, tunic, and trousers made of gray green wool.

This soldier demonstrates his strength by holding up three of his comrades.

The mustached solider in this studio photo wears an issued gray green wool Model 1909 tunic, as well as a gray green wool Model 1915 field cap. The number 81 stitched to his field cap indicates his unit.

The soldier in this studio photo wears a cotton tunic with gray green wool trousers. He has placed his gray green wool Model 1915 field cap (*Cupolino*) on a fur rug covering a table top.

The soldier (*soldato*) in this studio photo poses confidently wearing his gray green wool field tunic (*Giacca*) and cap (*Berretto*). The number 37 stitched above the leather visor and chinstrap of his field cap indicates his unit.

The soldier (*soldato*) in this studio photo poses proudly wearing his gray green (*grigioverde*) wool tunic (*Giacca*) and trousers (*Pantaloni*). He has placed his field cap (*Berretto*) on his folded overcoat. He has the number 41 stitched to his *berretto*, which indicates his unit.

Leaning confidently on a pedestal, this dark haired soldier poses proudly for a studio photo wearing his issued gray green wool tunic and trousers. The numbers 911 stitched to his field cap indicate his unit.

This soldier wears an issued Model 1909 tunic, as well as issued trousers and puttees made of gray green wool. His footwear appears to have come direct from the supply depot, as well.

This goateed soldier (*soldato*) wears a Model 1909 gray green (*grigioverde*) wool field tunic (*Giacca*) with five pointed metal star insignia fastened to the collar. The pads on the ends of his shoulders kept his rifle sling from slipping off.

The mustached soldier in this studio photo wears a tunic and trousers made of cotton. Such uniforms were preferred by many soldiers, particularly those serving in Libya.

This soldier wears a cotton field tunic with gray green (*grigioverde*) wool pants. Cotton was preferred, because it was easier than wool to launder and maintain.

This soldier (*soldato*) wears an issued Model 1909 gray green tunic with five-pointed metal star (*Stellette*) collar insignia fastened to his collar. He has chosen to tuck his pants (*Pantaloni*) into his field boots (*Scarpe*), instead of wrapping his legs with puttees (*Fasce mollettiere*). In addition, he has a pair of goggles (*Occhiali*) on his Model 1909 gray green wool field cap (*Berretto*).

This soldier wears a gray green wool field tunic and cap. Collar patches with vertical bars, such as his, were usually worn by machinegunners.

With his arm resting on a pedestal, this young soldier poses proudly in this studio photo wearing an issued Model 1909 tunic. The pads on the ends of his shoulder kept his rifle from slipping off.

This mustached soldier poses confidently with two ladies wearing his gray green wool Model 1909 field tunic. There is something about a man in uniform!

The mustached Major (*Maggiore*) seated in this late war vintage studio photo poses proudly wearing a privately tailored gray green wool tunic (*Giacca*) with a decoration ribbon (*Nastrino*).

Leaning on a pedestal, this mustached soldier poses for a studio photo wearing a Model 1909 gray green wool tunic with rank stripes stitched atop his cuffs. The crown and the number 30 stitched to his Model 1909 field cap indicate his unit.

This dark haired soldier (*soldato*) wears an issued gray green wool tunic (*Giacca*) with five-pointed metal star (*Stellette*) insignia fastened to the collar. He wears a neck wrap, which kept the coarse wool of his tunic from chafing.

With left hand on a pedestal, and his right hand on his hip, this mustached soldier poses confidently for a late war vintage studio photo wearing a gray green wool tunic and canvas trousers.

This soldier (*soldato*) poses proudly for a photo in a wooded area near the front, wearing a privately tailored gray green wool tunic (*Giacca*) with double breast pockets.

Clad in canvas and wool tunics, nine soldiers (*soldati*) pause for a photo while preparing an Italian cuisine using their issued mess equipment.

Wearing a variety of both privately tailored, as well as issued field tunics and caps, this group of soldiers poses confidently for a late war vintage photo.

Clad in barracks fatigues as well as field tunics, 15 soldiers (*soldati*) pause from enjoying their meal served in their mess equipment for a group photo.

Eleven soldiers (*soldati*) pose for a photo in front of a doorway wearing various styles of gray green (*grigioverde*) wool tunics and field caps.

Five soldiers pose confidently wearing gray green wool tunics and trousers. In addition to having five pointed metal star insignia fastened to their collars, they have metal insignia fastened to their shoulder straps, as well.

With their commanding officers clad in gray green (*grigioverde*) wool field tunics and caps, this group of soldiers poses proudly wearing their cotton fatigues.

Wearing various cuts of early to late war styles of tunics, seven soldiers pose for a photo with their canine companion. An eagle badge on the sleeve of the tunic indicated one was a naval aviator.

Seven soldiers pose for a photo with their canine companion wearing various cuts of early to late war styles of tunics. An eagle badge on the sleeve of the tunic indicated one was a naval aviator.

Five soldiers (*soldati*) pose confidently outside of a fortress wearing gray green (*grigioverde*) wool tunics and brownish gray field caps.

The soldier in this late war vintage studio photo wears a privately tailored pleated breast pocketed gray green wool tunic. This photo offers detail of the stitching on the leather ammo bandolier.

The soldier seated in this studio photo wears a Model 1909 gray green wool tunic with five pointed metal star collar insignia fastened to his collar. In addition, he wears tapered wool pants with no puttees and privately purchased boots.

In a wooded area near the front, three soldiers poses proudly for a photo wearing gray green wool field tunics and trousers.

The officer (*Ufficiale*) on the left wears a privately tailored double breast and side pocketed light colored gray green wool tunic, while his comrade on the right wears an issued Model 1909 tunic. Both wear field caps styled after the Model 1909.

The soldier in this studio photo wears a coarse gray green wool field tunic (*Giacca*) and cap (*Berretto*). The insignia stitched on his *berretto* was normally characteristic for volunteers.

Wrapped up in his gray green wool cloak, this mustached soldier (*soldato*) poses confidently for a studio photo wearing a gray green (*grigioverde*) wool field cap (*Berretto*) with leather chinstrap and visor.

This mustached staff officer is clad in a privately tailored pleated breast pocketed gray green wool field tunic, as well as a privately made cap with a leather visor and chin strap.

The infantry soldier in this studio photo poses proudly wearing a double breast pocketed gray green wool tunic and baggy trousers.

The soldier seated in this studio photo holds the rank of *caporale* (roughly the equivalent of corporal), as the chevrons on his gray green wool tunic indicate. In addition, he has a decoration ribbon stitched above his left breast pocket.

The dark haired soldier (*soldato*) in this studio photo is wrapped in a gray green (*grigioverde*) wool cloak (*Mantellina*) with cloth five pointed star (*Stellette*) insignia stitched to the collar. The star insignia fastened to the collar of his tunic is made of metal.

Seated on a stool with his elbow resting on a cushion covering a table, this soldier poses for a photo wearing a gray green wool field tunic and cap, as well as a pair of baggy pants with puttees wrapping the ends.

The infantryman holding a pair of leather gloves in this studio photo poses confidently in his privately tailored double breast and side pocketed gray green wool (*grigioverde*) field tunic (*Giacca*).

The enlisted rank (*Fante*) soldier featured in this studio photo taken in Brescia wears an issued gray green wool Model 1909 field tunic. He has covered his collar to protect his neck from the coarse wool of his tunic.

The mustached solider (*soldato*) in this studio poses confidently wearing his gray green (*grigioverde*) wool Model 1909 field tunic (*Giacca*) with a matching pair of pants (*Pantaloni*). In addition, he wears Model 1912 infantry boots with laces.

The infantryman in this late war vintage studio photo wears a privately tailored double breast pocketed gray green (*grigioverde*) wool tunic (*Giacca*) with brass buttons. His *grigioverde* wool field cap (*Berretto*) with shiny leather visor and chinstrap has a stiff construction.

This infantryman poses proudly wearing a double breast pocketed gray green wool tunic with matching pants and puttees. The lanyard around his neck is attached to his holstered sidearm.

With his hands in the pockets of his gray green wool trousers, this soldier poses confidently wearing a fitted tunic made of the same grade and color of wool. Also, visible is the leather scabbard of his bayonet with brass fittings.

The soldier seated in this studio photo wears a gray green (*grigioverde*) wool tunic (*Giacca*) with a decoration ribbon (*Nastrino*) stitched above his left breast pocket, and five pointed metal star (*Stelletta*) insignia fastened to his collar.

Six soldiers clad in gray green wool field tunics and trousers pose for a photo, with each having a look of determination on his face. All are *granatieri* (grenadiers), as their cloth collar and cap insignia indicates.

Eight soldiers (*soldati*) pose confidently wearing issued gray green (*grigioverde*) wool tunics with five pointed metal star (*Stellette*) collar insignia.

The mustached soldier in this studio photo wears a gray green wool Model 1909 field tunic with a classic issue cut. The pads on the ends of shoulders kept his rifle sling from slipping, especially when on a rigorous march.

This bearded soldier wears a gray green (*grigioverde*) wool tunic (*Giacca*) with matching trousers.

This *caporale maggiore* (roughly the equivalent of a corporal) poses with a tripod mounted observation instrument wearing a gray green wool tunic and leather ammo bandolier. The Italian captions written on this photo indicate it was taken in a region in Northeastern Italy known as Carnia Giulia. Also, the dates 1-2-3 November are the dates of the glorious advances of the Italian army.

The officer in this late war vintage studio photo wears a privately tailored gray green (*grigioverde*) wool tunic (*Giacca*) with pleated breast pockets. He rests his hands on his Model 1888 saber (*Sciabola*).

This solider wears a privately tailored double breast pocketed gray green wool tunic with trousers and puttees.

The solider holding his brass tipped leather bayonet scabbard wears an issue gray green (*grigioverde*) wool Model 1909 tunic. His *grigioverde* wool pants and puttees appear issued, as well.

With his right hand on a banister, this soldier poses proudly wearing a gray green wool field tunic and trousers. He has unit insignia stitched above the leather visor and chinstrap of his field cap.

The soldier holding a pair of leather gloves and wearing a gray green wool field tunic is armed with a bayonet (*Baionetta*). The spurs (*Speroni*) on his field boots (*Scarpe*) indicate he is in a mounted unit.

The soldier with his left hand resting on a table, and his right hand holding a riding crop, wears a tight fitting privately tailored tunic with double breast pockets. In addition, he wears a leather ammo bandolier.

The officer (*Ufficiale*) seated in this studio photo wears a privately tailored doubled pocketed field tunic (*Giacca*) made from a coarse grade of gray green (*grigioverde*) wool. He has a decoration ribbon (*Nastrino*) stitched above his left breast pocket, and unit insignia stitched to his sleeves.

The two dark haired soldiers (*soldati*) seated in this studio photo wear issued gray green (*grigioverde*) wool tunics with five pointed metal star insignia fastened to their collars.

This mustached soldier holding a pair of binoculars (*Binocolo*) wears a privately tailored double breast pocketed cotton field tunic, which he has belted with a single pronged leather belt. The lanyard around his neck fastens to his holstered sidearm.

Holding a walking stick in his right hand, this *caporale* poses proudly for a photo wearing a gray green (*grigioverde*)wool field tunic and trousers.

The officer (*Ufficiale*) featured in this studio photo wears a privately tailored gray green wool field tunic (*Giacca*) with five-pointed star (*Stellette*) insignia fastened to his collar and shoulder straps (*Spalline*). His has a decoration ribbon (*Nastrino*) stitched above the left breast pocket of his tunic.

The infantryman in this oval shaped studio photo wears a privately tailored double breast pocketed gray green (*grigioverde*) wool field tunic (*Giacca*). He has unit and rank insignia stitched to his *grigioverde* wool field cap (*Berretto*). His rank is lieutenant (*Tenente*).

Ten mustached soldiers (*soldati*) pose proudly for a late war vintage studio photo wearing gray green (*grigioverde*) wool tunics and pants. The two soldiers seated on the bench wear *grigioverde* wool field caps (*berretti*).

The soldier in this studio photo wears a privately tailored tunic made from a fine grade of green gray wool. He has a decoration ribbon (*Nastrino*) stitched to the breast of his tunic, as well as five pointed metal star (*Stellette*) insignia stitched to his collar.

The mustached soldier in this late war vintage studio photo has rank and unit distinctions stitched to privately purchased gray green (*grigioverde*) wool field cap (*Berretto*). In addition, he wears a privately tailored *grigioverde* wool tunic (*Giacca*) with pleated breast pockets. His rank is Captain (*Capitano*).

This late war vintage photo shows a mixture of soldiers who will be returning home, and who will be returning to the front lines.

Nine distinguished looking officers pose for a late war vintage photo wearing privately tailored gray green (*grigioverde*) wool field tunics. Each officer has rank and unit insignia stitched to his privately purchased field cap (*Berretto*).

In this studio, seven officers pose confidently wearing privately tailored gray green wool tunics. The graying officer seated in the center has several decoration ribbons stitched above the left breast pocket of his tunic.

These seven soldiers (*soldati*) pose proudly wearing a variety of tunics. The number 72 on their field caps (*Berretti*) indicates their unit.

Fourteen mustached soldiers (*soldati*) pose for a late war vintage photo wearing a variety of tunics and field caps. The soldier seated near the center holds a cane and a dispatch case.

This group of soldiers clad in canvas fatigues pauses for a group photo while on maneuvers. The white covers some are wearing over their field caps (*Berretti*) were normally worn only during maneuvers.

Twelve soldiers pose proudly for a studio photo wearing gray green (*grigioverde*) wool tunics with five pointed metal star (*Stellette*) insignia fastened to their collars.

The mustached soldier in this studio photo taken in Mondovi-Breo wears an issued gray green wool field tunic and trousers. The number 34 on his field cap (*Berretto*) indicates his unit.

Seven soldiers (*soldati*) clad in gray green (*grigioverde*) wool tunics and trousers pose for a photo with mountains in the background. Two of these soldiers have a Model 1915 field cap, which was referred to as either a *scodellino* or *cupolino*.

This group of soldiers poses for a photo wearing a variety of green gray wool and heavy cotton tunics. The officer in the center wears a privately tailored double breast pocket wool tunic, and is armed with a holstered Model 1915 Beretta semiautomatic pistol.

Twelve soldiers (*soldati*) clad in a variety of gray green (*grigioverde*) wool field tunics and caps pose for a group photo in a clearing near the frontlines.

The soldier on the left wears an issued gray green wool tunic, while his comrades are clad in cotton canvas tunics. All three wear gray green wool field caps (*Berretti*) with leather visors and chinstraps. Their artillery piece is directly behind them.

The high ranking mustached officer (*Ufficiale*) in this late war vintage studio photo wears a privately tailored double breast pocketed gray green (*grigioverde*) wool tunic (*Giacca*) and trousers.

In this oval shaped studio photo, a mustached soldier poses proudly wearing an issued gray green wool tunic with a decoration ribbon (*Nastrino*). He wears a high collar shirt to prevent the coarse wool of his tunic from rubbing against his neck.

The mustached infantryman in this studio photo wears an issued Model 1909 *grigioverde* (gray green) wool tunic with pads on the ends of his shoulders to keep his rifle sling from slipping off. The number 72 stitched to his *berretto* (field cap) indicates his unit.

With their hands resting on a pedestal, two young soldiers pose proudly for a photo wearing gray green wool field tunics and trousers.

The mustached grenadier in this studio photo wears an issued Model 1909 gray green wool tunic with five pointed metal star and cloth grenadier insignia on his collar. He has placed his gray green wool Model 1909 field cap on a pedestal, which bears grenadier insignia, as well.

This mustached soldier pauses in the middle of a street for a photo wearing a gray green (*grigioverde*) wool field tunic, cap, and cloak.

This soldier poses for a photo with his canine companion wearing a well worn gray green wool tunic and trousers.

The dark haired, mustached soldier in this studio photo wears an issued Model 1909 gray green wool tunic with beige cotton pants and gray green wool puttees.

The gloved officer (*Ufficiale*) in this studio photo wears a privately tailored double breast pocketed gray green (*grigioverde*) wool tunic with decoration ribbon (*Nastrino*), as well as rank insignia on his cuffs.

This officer (*Ufficiale*) poses confidently in the middle of a town square wearing a privately tailored, double breast pocketed gray green (*grigioverde*) wool tunic (*Giacca*) with a double pronged buckle leather belt (*Cinturone*).

Six soldiers (*soldati*) pose confidently for a photo clad in various models of gray green (*grigioverde*) wool field tunics and caps. The number 83 stitched to their field caps (*Berretti*) indicates their unit. This photo is dated 1916.

These six soldiers (*soldati*) pose proudly in this studio photo wearing gray green wool tunics and trousers. They have cloth unit distinctions stitched to the sleeves of their tunics.

Four soldiers (*soldati*) pose for a photo before boarding their vehicle wearing gray green wool tunics and overcoats. This photo displays both the front and back sides of the overcoat collar.

Four soldiers (*soldati*) outfitted with gray green (*grigioverde*) wool tunics, pants, and field caps enjoying conversation in mountainous terrain.

This mustached soldier poses for a photo with a small town in the background wearing a gray green (*grigioverde*) wool tunic, trousers, overcoat, and field cap.

Chapter Four

Armor and Motor Corps

This is a fabulous photo of a Fiat 2000 *Carro Armato* in 1917. It is armed with a 65mm cannon located in the turret, as well as seven 6.5mm machineguns. Weighing approximately 38 tons, and protected by 15mm to 20mm thick armor, the tank could reach a maximum speed of 6km per hour. The first Italian armored unit was formed in Verona, Italy.

Three motorists wearing gray green wool tunics and a mechanic in fatigues pause for a photo while their engine is repaired.

On a road en route to the front lines, four soldiers clad in gray green wool tunics and field caps pause for a photo with their vehicle before driving further.

Four soldiers pose for a photo wearing various models of gray green (*grigioverde*) wool field tunics and caps. Their Fiat 15ters are loaded with material for the front.

Salvaging a wrecked vehicle.

The driver behind the steering wheel is in the *2 Autoreparato*.

Six soldiers (*soldati*) pose for a photo with their Fiat 15ter wearing various models of gray green wool field tunics and caps. Motorists preferred heavy fleece coats, such as the one the soldier wearing the Model 1915 field cap has on, because of exposure to the elements.

These six soldiers wearing gray green wool and cotton tunics pose proudly with their Fiat 15ter. They have folded up the canopy that would cover the driver and passenger.

The driver of this spoke wheel vehicle poses for a photo while parked on the snow covered ground. This type of vehicle was often referred to as an *Autobus*.

With their vehicles parked in field, this group of soldiers clad in various models of field caps pauses for a meal and a photo.

This group of officers wearing gray green wool tunics and caps examine a wounded soldier before he is loaded into a Fiat *Ambulanza* (Ambulance).

Three officers wearing gray green (*grigioverde*) wool field tunics and caps pose for a photo with their vehicle parked on the coast.

Seated confidently in their spoke wheeled vehicle, these four soldiers pose for a photo dressed in gray green wool field tunics.

Eleven *Alpini* and two soldiers wearing gray green wool tunics and leather ammo bandoliers pose for a photo with their vehicles parked on rocky terrain.

The soldier behind the steering wheel of this spoke wheeled vehicle wears a cloth cap and gray green wool tunic.

Three officers wearing gray green wool field caps are driving past a building with arches, and a clay tile roof.

Four soldiers clad gray green (*grigioverde*) wool field tunics and caps pose for a photo with their vehicles.

With his left hand in his pocket, this mustached *caporale* (roughly the equivalent of a corporal) poses for a studio photo wearing a gray green (*grigioverde*) wool field tunic (*Giacca*) and cap (*Berretto*). He has stamped metal automobile (*Automobilisti*) insignia fastened to the sleeve of his tunic, as well as on his cap.

The soldier with his arms crossed in this studio photo wears a gray green wool field tunic and cap. He has unit insignia stitched to his shoulder straps (PA is *Parco Automobilisti*) and his sleeve. In addition, he has a decoration ribbon (*Nastrino*) stitched above his left pocket, where he has placed a pen.

The driver in this 1915 vintage studio photo wears a gray green (*grigioverde*) wool overcoat and field cap. He has metal automobile (*Automobilisti*) fastened to his field cap.

The *caporale* (roughly the equivalent of a corporal) in this studio photo holding his gloves wears a double breast pocketed cotton field tunic and baggy pants. He has metal *Automobilisti* fastened to his dark colored wool field cap.

The soldier in this studio wears a gray green wool field cap with automobile insignia. In addition, he wears a leather ammo bandolier.

The mustached driver in this studio photo holding his gloves wears a gray green (*grigioverde*) wool overcoat with a fur collar. His *grigioverde* field cap (*Berretto*) bears metal automobile insignia.

A line of trucks filled with troops headed for the front lines.

A group of soldiers wearing helmets and field caps freeing a self-propelled artillery piece stuck on a muddy road.

Chapter Five

Artillery

(Artiglieria)

Two *k.u.k Soldaten* (imperial and royal Austro-Hungarian soldiers/troopers) examine a captured Italian heavy artillery piece to see if it can be reused.

One of many abandoned trench mortars (*bombarde*) on the Piave.

A group of *k.u.k Soldaten* (imperial and royal Austro-Hungarian soldiers/troopers) transporting captured Italian coastal artillery.

These two cast iron turrets protect artillery positions in the Dolomite mountains.

An abandoned howitzer in the Dolomite mountains.

This field cannon has been mounted on a rotating platform in order to be used for anti-aircraft purposes.

A group of artillerists clad in canvas tunics and wool field caps prepares to transport their caissons.

This group of artillerists wearing canvas fatigues and wool field caps is towing their field cannon up a wooded hillside.

Wearing a gray green (*grigioverde*) colored helmet and field tunic (*Giacca*), this artillerist poses for a photo between two heavy caliber projectiles.

A group of artillerists clad in cotton fatigues and wool field caps struggling to transport their howitzer higher in the mountains.

This group of artillerists pauses for a photo with their howitzers on a mountain road wearing cotton fatigues and wool field caps. The strong artillerist holding the barrel of the howitzer in this photo displays the barrel markings.

A group of artillerists dressed in cotton fatigues and wool field caps prepare to fire their howitzer on a mountain road.

Beside a sandbagged position, a group of artillerists wearing gray green (*grigioverde*) wool field caps (*Berretti*) pose proudly with their 305mm caliber howitzer.

A group of artillerists preparing to fire at incoming aircraft. This photo also shows how artillery rounds were transported.

Three rugged artillerists pose for a photo with their deeply entrenched 305mm caliber howitzer.

Three sailors pose for a photo with their naval cannon.

In this 1918 vintage photo, a group of soldiers wearing gray green wool field tunics pose for a photo in muddy trenches with their heavy caliber mortar.

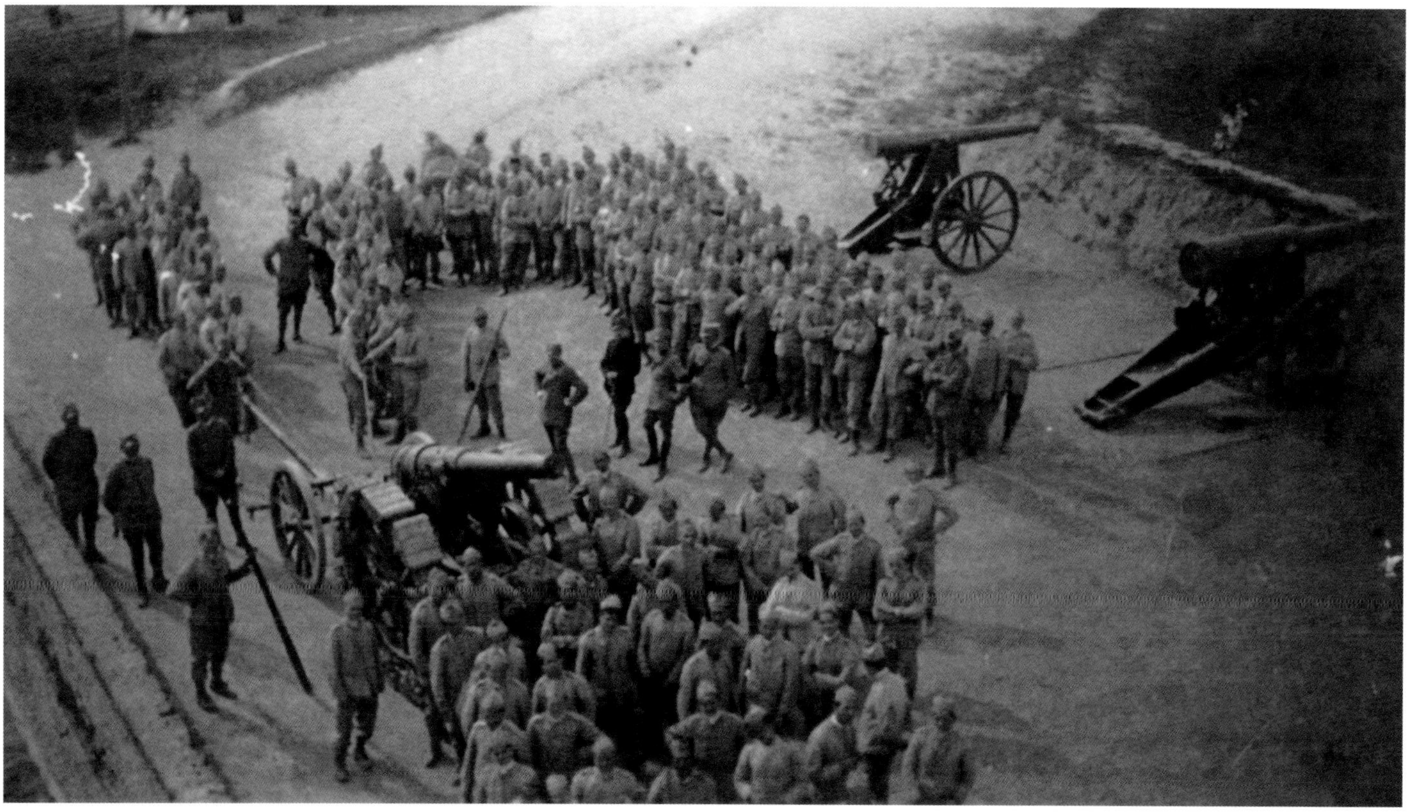

A large group of artillerists poses for a photo with their fortress artillery pieces.

Ten artillerists clad in gray green wool field tunics and cotton fatigues pose confidently for a photo with their 75mm caliber Model 1911 Deport field cannon. All have crossed cannon insignia on their field caps.

Five relaxing artillerists pose for a photo with their heavy caliber mortar in a wooded area.

Four artillerists clad in gray green (*grigioverde*) wool uniforms pose for a photo with their heavy caliber artillery piece.

Nine artillerists dressed in various models and makes of gray green wool field tunics and caps pose proudly for a photo on and around their field cannon.

Transporting heavy artillery to the front.

In addition to the field cannon in this candid photo are a regimental priest, as well as Italian and Serbian officers and enlisted rank soldiers.

A mustached soldier wearing a gray green wool field tunic and cap poses for a photo seated behind his field cannon. This photo was taken in Albania.

A heavy caliber mortar in a concealed position.

Five artillerists clad in gray green wool field tunics and caps pose for a photo with their field cannon.

These five artillerists wearing gray green (*grigioverde*) Model 1915 Adrian steel helmets and field tunics pose for a photo behind their 75mm caliber Model 1911 Deport field cannon.

This group of artillerists poses behind their field cannon in a fortified position.

A group of artillerists wearing a variety of gray green wool tunics and field caps pause for a photo with their heavy caliber mortar.

Two mustached artillerists outfitted with gray green wool uniforms and goggles with tinted lenses pose for a photo with their howitzer.

A captured 280mm caliber mortar is on display in a park. The designation on the side reads *Per Obice da 280 Corto*. Projectiles for this weighed 215kg.

This *k.u.k*, or imperial and royal Austro-Hungarian soldier, poses proudly in a warehouse full of captured Italian naval cannons. Trieste, July 1916.

Ten artillerists wearing gray green (*grigioverde*) wool field caps pose for a photo with their two howitzers.

A group of artillerists clad in pre to early war uniforms preparing to fire their 75mm caliber Model 1911 Deport.

Firing a 75mm caliber Model 1911 Deport.

One of many abandoned trench mortars (*bombarde*) on the Isonzo.

The artillerist holding his saber in this studio photo wears a gray green (*grigioverde*) wool field tunic (*Giacca*) and cap (*Berretto*) with a leather ammo bandolier.

Holding a riding crop, this artillerist poses for a late war vintage studio photo wearing a privately tailored, double breast pocketed gray green (*grigioverde*) wool tunic and trousers, along with a leather ammo bandolier.

The artillerist in this studio photo wears a gray green wool field cap with crossed cannon unit insignia stitched to both his leather chinstrap and visor. In addition, he is outfitted with a leather ammo bandolier.

*With his right hand holding a cigarette, and his left hand holding his saber, this artillerist poses proudly wearing a gray green (*grigioverde*) wool field cap (*Berretto*) and tunic (*Giacca*) with leather ammo bandolier. The spurs (*Speroni*) on his boots indicate he is in a mounted or horse drawn artillery unit (*Artiglieria a cavallo*).*

Holding his gloves and saber, this artillerist poses for a late war vintage photo wearing a gray green wool field cap, tunic, and pants. His high collar cotton shirt kept the coarse wool of his tunic from rubbing his neck.

The artillerist in this studio photo wears a privately tailored pleated pocketed gray green (*grigioverde*) field tunic (*Giacca*) with a decoration ribbon (*Nastrino*) stitched above his left breast pocket.

Standing on a fur rug in this studio photo is an artillerist dressed in a privately tailored, pleated pocketed, gray green wool field tunic with brass buttons. His field cap bearing crossed cannon insignia was privately made, as well.

The artillerist in this late war vintage studio photo wears a privately tailored gray green wool (*grigioverde*) tunic with external pockets and brass buttons. He has metal crossed cannon insignia fastened to his field cap.

Chapter Six

Cavalry and Mounted Troops

The two young soldiers in this studio photo have unique covers over their headdress. The young dragoon, wearing a black wool uniform on the left, has covered his Model 1910 Dragoon helmet with ornate paper.

This mustached dragoon, holding his saber in this pre to early war studio photo, wears a black wool uniform with rank stripes on his cuffs. In addition, he wears a Model 1910 Dragoon helmet, or *Dragone M1910*.

With his hands resting on his saber (*Sciabola*), this mustached dragoon poses proudly dressed in a black wool tunic with brass buttons in this pre to early war vintage studio photo. He wears a *Dragone M1910 Elmo*, or a Model 1910 Dragoon helmet.

This mustached dragoon wears a Model 1910 Dragoon helmet, and a black wool tunic with brass buttons. He is armed with a saber (*Sciabola*).

The dragoon in this studio photo taken in Brescia wears a Model 1910 Dragoon helmet, and a black wool tunic with brass buttons. This pre to early war vintage cabinet portrait offers a side view of the Model 1910 helmet.

The lancer in this pre to early vintage studio wears a *Colbacco* (cylindrically shaped headdress made of fur or felt) with a white cover bearing the number 2. White covers were usually worn over a soldier's headdress during maneuvers.

The mustached cavalryman holding his saber in this pre to early war studio photo wears a black wool tunic with brass buttons.

In this pre to early war vintage studio photo, the cavalryman holding his headdress (*Colbacco*) in his right hand and his saber (*Sciabola*) in his left wears a black wool tunic with cavalry distinctions on his collar.

The mounted artillerist in this studio photo wears a black wool tunic and plumed headdress with crossed cannon insignia. His left hand holds his saber with sword knot.

The mustached cavalryman in this pre to early war vintage studio photo wears a black wool tunic and trousers. He has placed his headdress on an ornately crafted pedestal.

Holding the reigns of his horse, this young *caporale* (roughly the equivalent of a corporal) poses proudly wearing a gray green (*grigioverde*) wool field tunic (*Giacca*) and cap (*Berretto*).

This soldier poses proudly on his horse wearing a gray green wool field tunic, cap, and trousers.

A group of lancers (*lancieri*) form a line, and prepare to repel an attack.

This soldier poses proudly on his horse wearing a gray green (*grigioverde*) wool uniform.

With his hands on his saber (*Sciabola*) and his headdress (*Colbacco*) on the table next to him, this cavalryman poses for a late war vintage studio photo wearing a gray green wool tunic and trousers.

The mustached officer holding his saber in this late war vintage studio photo wears a privately tailored gray green wool uniform with a leather ammo bandolier. The lanyard around his neck attaches to his holstered sidearm.

The soldier in this oval shaped studio photo wears a double breast pocketed gray green (*grigioverde*) wool tunic with five pointed metal star (*Stellette*) insignia fastened to his collar.

The lancer in this studio photo wears a gray green wool tunic with a leather ammo bandolier. The type of field cap he is wearing is known as a *capello a visera a due punte* (two-pointed forage/tent cap with a visor).

This soldier poses proudly for a photo with his horse wearing a gray green (*grigioverde*) wool field tunic and cap.

Dragoons, 1914.

The officer jumping with his horse in this pre to early war photograph wears a black wool uniform.

Chapter Seven

Alpine Troops

(Alpini)

Seven *Alpini* pose for a photo in mountainous terrain with their belt fed machinegun mounted on a tripod.

The *Alpino* in this studio photo wears a gray green wool tunic and felt *cappello* (*Alpini* field cap) with an eagle feather in the pompom holder. He has a leather ammo bandolier flung over his left shoulder. Alpini were nicknamed "*penne nere*," or black feathers.

This *Alpino* wears a gray green (*grigioverde*) felt *cappello* (*Alpini* field cap), and an issued wool tunic with technical/communication unit insignia stitched to his sleeve.

This *Alpino* wears a privately tailored, pleated pocketed gray green wool field tunic with brass buttons and rank chevrons stitched to his cuffs. He has removed the eagle feather from his *cappello* (*Alpini* field cap) for this studio photo.

With his hand resting on a pedestal, this *Alpino* poses proudly for a studio photo wearing a gray green (*grigioverde*) felt *cappello* (*Alpini* field cap), and a wool tunic with pleated pockets.

In this studio photo, the *Alpino* dressed in an issued gray green wool tunic has placed his felt *cappello* (*Alpini* field cap) with eagle feather on a pedestal.

The *Alpino* with the rank of *caporale maggiore* wears a gray green wool Model 1909 field tunic with baggy pants. He has an eagle feather in the pompom holder stitched to the leather band of his *cappello* (*Alpini* field cap).

This *Alpino* wears a gray green (*grigioverde*) pleated breast pocketed wool field tunic and felt *cappello* (*Alpini* field cap). The lanyard around his neck attaches to his holstered sidearm.

The *Alpino* seated in this studio photo wears a gray green (*grigioverde*) pleated breast pocketed wool field tunic and felt *cappello* (*Alpini* field cap). In addition, the lanyard around his neck attaches to his holstered sidearm, and he has removed the eagle feather from his *cappello*.

The *Alpino* in this studio photo holding his gloves with his saber (*Sciabola*) tucked under his arm wears a pleated pocketed gray green (*grigioverde*) wool field tunic with baggy pants, which he has bloused out over his puttees (*mollettiere*). He has an eagle feather in his felt *cappello* (*Alpini* field cap).

The confident looking *Alpino* in this studio photo wears a felt *cappello* (*Alpini* field cap) bearing his unit distinction, and an issued field tunic with five pointed star (*Stellette*) insignia fastened to his collar.

With an eagle feather in his *cappello* (*Alpini* field cap), this *Alpino* poses proudly for a photo wearing a privately tailored gray green (*grigioverde*) wool field tunic with brass buttons and five pointed star (*Stellette*) insignia fastened to his collar.

Two *Alpini* pose confidently for a studio photo clad in privately tailored, pleated pocketed gray green wool tunics.

The *Alpino* posed in this studio photo is dressed in an issued gray green (*grigioverde*) wool Model 1909 field tunic and a felt *cappello* (*Alpini* field cap).

The confident *Alpino* in this studio photo wears a gray green felt *cappello* (*Alpini* field cap) with an eagle feather and pleated pocketed wool field tunic with brass buttons.

This *Alpino* wears a privately tailored pleated pocketed gray green (*grigioverde*) wool field tunic. He has placed his *cappello* (*Alpini* field cap) with eagle feather on the table in this studio photo.

Six *Alpini* clad in gray green (*grigioverde*) field tunics pose for a photo with their canine friend.

This group of *Alpini* poses for a photo with their artillery pieces wearing gray green wool tunics and leather ammo bandoliers.

Five *Alpini* pose proudly for a photo with soldiers from other branches of the armed forces.

A group of armed *Alpini* clad in gray green (*grigioverde*) wool uniforms poses proudly for a photo in a village near the front.

With his hand resting on a pedestal, the mustached *Alpino* in this studio photo poses confidently wearing an issued gray green wool Model 1909 tunic and trousers. He wears an eagle feather on his *cappello* (*Alpini* field cap).

This *Alpino* resting on a pile of stones poses for a photo wearing a gray green (*grigioverde*) wool tunic and felt *cappello* (*Alpini* field cap).

Alpini pose for a group photo with their comrades from other branches of the armed forces.

This *Alpino* dressed in a gray green wool Model 1909 tunic and felt *cappello* (*Alpini* field cap) is prepared to go to battle with not only his bolt action rifle (*Fucile*) and bayonet (*Baionetta*), but with his musical instrument, as well.

In this studio photo, an *Alpino* poses proudly wearing a gray green (*grigioverde*) wool tunic and felt *cappello* (*Alpini* field cap).

These four *Alpini* clad in gray green wool uniforms pause for a photo while enjoying a drink. The spectator under the table holds a trench lantern.

Three *Alpini* wearing gray green (*grigioverde*) wool tunics and pants pose for a photo with a child. Each *Alpino* wears a felt *cappello* (*Alpini* field cap).

Alpini transporting a howitzer high into the Dolomite mountains.

At an elevation of 2000 meters, three *Alpini* in deep snow prepare to fire their belt fed machinegun (*mitragliatrice*).

Three *Alpini* dressed in gray green (*grigioverde*) wool uniforms pose for a photo with three of their comrades from other branches of the Italian armed forces.

Chapter Eight

Arditi

(Fearless/Audacious Assault Troops)

This dark haired *Ardito* poses proudly for a late war vintage studio photo wearing a gray green wool field tunic with decoration ribbon. He is armed with a holstered side arm and trench knife/dagger.

Arditi and their comrades from other branches of the armed forces pose for a late war vintage photo wearing a variety of headdresses and tunics.

A group of *Arditi* dressed in various models of field caps and tunic pose for a late war vintage photo with civilians.

Two *Arditi* pose proudly for a late war vintage photo with a woman and child.

A mustached *Ardito* poses proudly for a late war vintage studio photo wearing a gray green (*grigioverde*) wool uniform. He has cloth unit insignia stitched to the sleeve of his tunic. He is a soldier of *Truppa D Assalto Fiamme Verdi- Arditi Alpini*. Note he wears his insignia incorrectly.

Chapter Nine

Bersaglieri

(Elite/Guard Troops)

A group of *Bersaglieri* pauses from enjoying a meal in their mess kits for a photo. The *Bersagliere* standing on the left wears a *moretto* (plumed *Bersaglieri* headdress) and has machinegunner insignia stitched to the sleeve of his gray green wool tunic.

The mustached *Bersagliere* in this studio photo wears a gray green wool Model 1909 field tunic and plumed headdress known as a *moretto*. He has covered his *moretto* with a cotton cover.

This *Bersagliere* wears a plumed *moretto* and a gray green (*grigioverde*) wool tunic with pleated breast pockets. The plumes of the *moretto* were referred to in Italian as *Piumetto*.

Wearing a plumed *moretto* and gray green wool tunic (*Giacca*), pants (*Pantaloni*) and puttees (*Mollettiere*), this *Bersagliere* poses for a photo with his female companion.

This *Bersagliere* wears an issued gray green (*grigioverde*) wool Model 1909 field tunic and a plumed *moretto*. The pads on the ends of his shoulders kept his rifle from slipping off.

This *Bersagliere* wears a plumed *moretto* and a gray green wool tunic with five pointed metal star collar insignia. His field boots were the model preferred by *Bersaglieri* when available at the depot.

The mustached *Bersagliere* in this shadowy studio photo wears a gray green wool cloak and a plumed *moretto*.

This *Bersagliere* wears a plumed *moretto* and a privately tailored gray green wool tunic with external pockets. He has *ciclista* or cyclist insignia stitched on the sleeve of his tunic.

This mustached *Bersagliere* posed here in this pre to early war vintage studio photo wears a plumed *moretto* and dark wool tunic (*Giacca*) with cotton pants (*Pantaloni*).

This *Bersaglieri* officer wears a privately tailored gray green wool tunic with pleated breast pockets. He has a cover over his plumed *moretto* to both camouflage and protect it from exposure.

This mustached *Bersagliere* wears a plumed *moretto* and a gray green (*grigioverde*) wool tunic (*Giacca*) with five pointed star (*Stellette*) collar insignia.

This *Bersagliere* wears a gray green (*grigioverde*) wool tunic and a plumed *moretto*.

A fully equipped *Bersagliere ciclista*.

Posing proudly, this *Bersagliere* wears a plumed *moretto* with cloth cover and a gray green wool tunic which he has belted with a leather belt (*Cinturone*) with brass buckle. This photo offers the details of the brass belt buckle.

Nine *Bersaglieri* in a wooded area outfitted with full battledress.

This is a commercially produced photo postcard depicting *Bersaglieri* forming a firing line. On the reverse side of this photo postcard is a postal stamp from Padova.

The mustached *Bersagliere* in this pre to early war vintage studio photo taken in Milan wears a plumed *moretto* and a dark wool tunic. The lanyard around his neck attaches his holstered sidearm.

The two *Bersaglieri* in this pre to early war vintage studio photo wear dark wool tunics and trousers. Each wears a plumed *moretto* and has lanyard around his neck attached to a holstered sidearm.

In this pre to early war vintage studio photo is a *Bersagliere* wearing a plumed *moretto* and a dark wool tunic with ornamental braids and frogs.

The mustached *Bersagliere* in this pre to early war vintage studio photo wears a plumed *moretto* and a dark wool tunic with five pointed star collar insignia. The lanyard around his neck attaches his holstered sidearm.

Three *Bersaglieri* clad in dark wool cloaks. Each wears a plumed *moretto*.

The young *Bersagliere* holding his gloves in this pre to early war vintage studio photo wears a dark wool tunic and plumed *moretto*. This photo was taken at a studio in Turin (*Torino*), Italy.

With his hand resting on an intricately carved chair, this mustached *Bersagliere* poses proudly wearing a plumed *moretto* and dark wool tunic with trousers.

This mustached *Bersagliere* poses proudly in this studio photo taken in Milan (*Milano*) wearing a plumed *moretto* and a gray green (*grigioverde*) wool field tunic with pleated breast pockets.

Bersaglieri ciclisti (bicyclists) line up for a photo wearing Model 1915 Adrian steel helmets with plumes and foreign manufactured gasmasks.

A pre to early war vintage photo of two *Bersaglieri*. Written in Italian on the photo is "*Cheers and hugs from your brother Oreste*". Oreste Pongiluppi is the great grand father of Professor Dr. Renato Zavattini.

Chapter Ten

Carabinieri

(Gendarme/Military Police)

This *Carabinieri* wears a black wool double breasted tunic with brass buttons and a cloak. He has placed his *lucerna* (*Carabinieri* headdress) on the table next to him.

This *Carabinieri* wearing a cloth cover over his *lucerna* (*Carabinieri* headdress) poses for a photo next to a floatplane with his comrades from other branches of the Italian armed forces.

Carabinieri, 1917.

Four *Carabinieri* in training.

Chapter Eleven

Life on the Front and in the Trenches

Four *soldati* (soldiers) clad in gray green wool uniforms take aim from their wooded position armed with 6.5 mm caliber Model 1891 Carcano bolt action rifles and a 9mm caliber Beretta semiautomatic pistol.

This group of soldiers clad in green gray (*grigioverde*) wool uniforms and helmets repel an attack from their fortified position.

This group of *soldati* (soldiers) pauses from their meal and camp activities for a photo. This photo offers a glimpse of what camp life was like for the Italian soldiers during the First World War.

A group of soldiers dressed in various models of field tunics and caps pose for a photo in a camp near the front lines.

This group of *soldati* (soldiers) poses for a photo on a hillside dressed in various models of gray green (*grigioverde*) wool tunics and field caps.

Soldiers from various branches of the Italian armed forces pause from eating a meal for a photo.

The bearded soldier (*soldato*) wearing a knitted gray green wool cap and overcoat with fur collar poses confidently for a photo holding a 6.5mm caliber Model 1891 Carcano bolt-action rifle in his gloved hands. He is also equipped with a binocular case and ammunition pouches. Written on the reverse side of this photo is "*1915 al fronte*."

Four officers dressed in privately tailored gray green (*grigioverde*) wool tunics poses for a photo at the corner of a building.

This group of *soldati* (soldiers) dressed in various models of field tunics and caps poses for a photo near a damaged building.

Twenty-nine *soldati* (soldiers) pose for a group photo clad in various models of field tunics and caps.

Five officers dressed in green gray (*grigioverde*) wool field tunics and caps pose for a photo with a stucco wall in the background.

While their comrade enjoys a shave, this fierce looking group of *soldati* (soldiers) poses for a photo armed with 6.5mm caliber Model 1891 Carcano bolt action rifles and Model 1889 revolvers.

Wearing various models of field caps, this bold group of soldiers poses for a photo armed with Model 1889 revolvers and 6.5mm caliber Model 1891 Carcano bolt action rifles in a wooded area.

The soldier (*soldato*) leaning on his walking stick wears a gray green wool uniform and Model 1915 Adrian steel helmet. He is equipped with a Model 1917 canteen and a Polivalente gasmask. This photo is dated 1917.

One *Alpino*, and two soldiers from other branches of the armed forces wearing gray green (*grigioverde*) wool uniforms, pose for a photo with a civilian.

Seven *soldati* (soldiers), wearing various models of cotton tunics and leather footwear, pose proudly in this late war vintage photo.

This group of soldiers clad in a myriad of field tunics and caps poses for a photo at the edge of a wood.

The soldier (*soldato*), wearing a gray green (*grigioverde*) wool field tunic (*Giacca*) and cap (*Berretto*), shows in this photo taken inside a bunker that he is ready for action armed with his 6.5mm caliber Model 1891 Carcano bolt action rifle with bayonet.

A group of *soldati* (soldiers) clad in gray green (*grigioverde*) uniforms prepares to receive communion during a mass in a small chapel on the coast.

These *soldati* (soldiers) from the 7th Regiment pause for a group photo while enjoying a drink from their Model 1907 wood canteens, as well as a meal for their mess kits. Most are wearing an early to mid-war style of wool gaiters, or spats.

Five officers dressed in gray green (*grigioverde*) wool field tunics and caps pose for a photo in a field near the front lines.

Two *soldati* (soldiers) clad in gray green wool field tunics and caps pose for a photo on a dirt road in Albania with one of the locals.

Alpini on skis hiking up a snow covered mountain.

Fortified positions in the Dolomite mountains.

Atop a snow covered mountain *Alpini* armed with 6.5mm caliber Model 1891 Carcano bolt action rifles and Fiat-Revelli Model 1914 machineguns prepare to engage advancing Austro-Hungarian forces.

Italian, French, and British NCOs and officers.

Seven *soldati* (soldiers) outfitted in privately tailored, as well as issued gray green (*grigioverde*) wool tunics.

This mustached soldier wears an issued gray green wool Model 1909 field tunic with pads on the ends of his shoulder. He has placed his gray green wool field cap with leather visor and chinstrap on a rock.

The soldier with a crown and number 7 stitched with black thread on his gray green (*grigioverde*) wool field cap wears an issued *grigioverde* wool Model 1909 field tunic with pants and puttees.

Equipped with four Model 1891 leather ammo pouches (*Giberna*), this *caporale* poses proudly wearing a gray green (*grigioverde*) wool tunic, trousers, and puttees.

Twenty-three *soldati* (soldiers) pose for a group photo at the edge of a wood wearing various models of *grigioverde* (gray green) wool field tunics and caps. Several have decoration bars stitched to their tunics.

High in the Dolomite mountains, a group of soldiers pose for a photo wearing gray green wool tunics, caps, cloaks, trousers, and puttees.

Three *soldati* (soldiers) in *grigioverde* (gray green) wool uniforms pose for a late war vintage photo with their canine friend on a bicycle.

Two officers and two chaplains converse at a railroad station.

This group of soldiers poses for a photo outside of their tents wearing various models of field tunics and caps.

Gathered outside of their barracks, soldiers wearing gray green field tunics, caps, and Model 1915 Adrian helmets pose for a photo with their canine friend while enjoying music and a drink.

This group of soldiers gathered outside their barracks pauses for a photo while eating meals from their mess kits.

This group of *soldati* (soldiers) poses for a photo clad in *grigioverde* (gray green) tunics, caps, and Model 1915 Adrian helmets.

Gathered in front of an iron gate, this group of soldiers armed with 6.5 mm caliber Model 1891 Carcano bolt action rifles wears a variety of field tunics and caps.

Constructing trenches, 1916.

Two officers wearing privately purchased gray green wool field tunics and caps converse with each other at their barracks.

This officer wearing a privately tailored *grigioverde* (gray green) wool uniform poses with his canine friend seated outside his barracks.

Drinking a toast inside a well stocked bunker.

A group of military bandsmen clad in gray green wool (*grigioverde*) field tunics and caps.

Five officers dressed in privately purchased gray green wool field tunics and caps. The officer in the center has a decoration ribbon (Nastrino) stitched above his left breast pocket.

Eleven *soldati* (soldiers) outfitted with gray green (*grigioverde*) wool field caps, overcoats, and cloaks pose for a group photo in a town near front lines. The mustached officer near the center of the group is equipped with a leather ammo bandolier.

In this humorously staged photo, five soldiers demonstrate restraining, as well as hand-to-hand combat techniques.

A group of soldiers at an observation post. The wood box on the stone wall next to the soldier wearing cotton fatigues contains a field telephone.

This group on maneuvers in the mountainous terrain of southern Europe wears cotton fatigues, as well as wool tunics and caps.

A child and a group of *soldati* (soldiers) wearing *grigioverde* (gray green) wool uniforms gather around a motorcycle for a photo.

This group of soldiers wearing gray green wool field caps and Model 1915 Adrian steel helmets pauses for a photo while enjoying a drink.

Waiting for an enemy to advance, 1917.

Eighteen soldiers clad in various models of gray green wool field tunics and caps pose for a late war vintage group photo. The *Alpino* on the far left wears a felt *cappello* (*Alpini* headdress).

A group of artillerists clad in cotton fatigues and wool field caps manning their cannons in a fortified position.

The officer (*Ufficiale*) on the right with the pair of binoculars around his neck wears a gray green wool field cap and cotton overcoat. The officer on the left wears a gray green wool tunic and overcoat.

A group of *soldati* (soldiers) dressed in gray green wool uniforms and cotton fatigues pose for a photo in a wooded area near the front.

Four soldiers dressed in *grigioverde* (gray green) wool uniforms pose for a photo in deep snow.

Three mustached *soldati* (soldiers) pose for a photo dressed in privately made gray green wool field tunics and caps.

This group of soldiers poses for a photo on a tree lined road dressed in gray green wool field tunics, caps, and cotton fatigues.

A group of *soldati* (soldiers) gathered around a table dressed in *grigioverde* (gray green) wool tunics pauses for a photo before resuming their discussion.

Celebrating Christmas at the barracks.

Ten soldiers clad in gray green wool field tunics and caps pause for a photo while enjoying a drink and a bite to eat.

These eight soldiers are ready for action dressed in their gray green wool uniforms and armed with the 6.5mm caliber Model 1891 Carcano bolt action rifles.

This group of soldiers pause for a photo before continuing to prepare a meal at their field kitchen with their mess equipment.

The three soldiers in this humorously staged photo demonstrate how ladles and bottles could be used in hand-to-hand combat when rifles and bayonets were not available.

The soldiers aboard these wooden skiffs are dressed in gray green wool field tunics, as well as caps, and are equipped with Model 1891 leather ammo pouches.

These soldiers are dressed in gray green wool uniforms and armed with 6.5mm caliber Model 1891 Carcano bolt action rifles.

This mustached soldier (*soldato*) pauses for a photo in a village near the front holding his privately purchased gray green (*grigioverde*) wool field cap (*Berretto*).

Six *soldati* (soldiers) dressed in *grigioverde* (gray green) wool tunics, caps, and cloaks pose for a photo.

This group of soldiers wearing gray green wool overcoats and Model 1915 Adrian steel helmets pauses for a photo with their horses and caissons while passing through a village en route to the frontlines.

A cluster of Italian soldiers at the foot of a mountain in Albania.

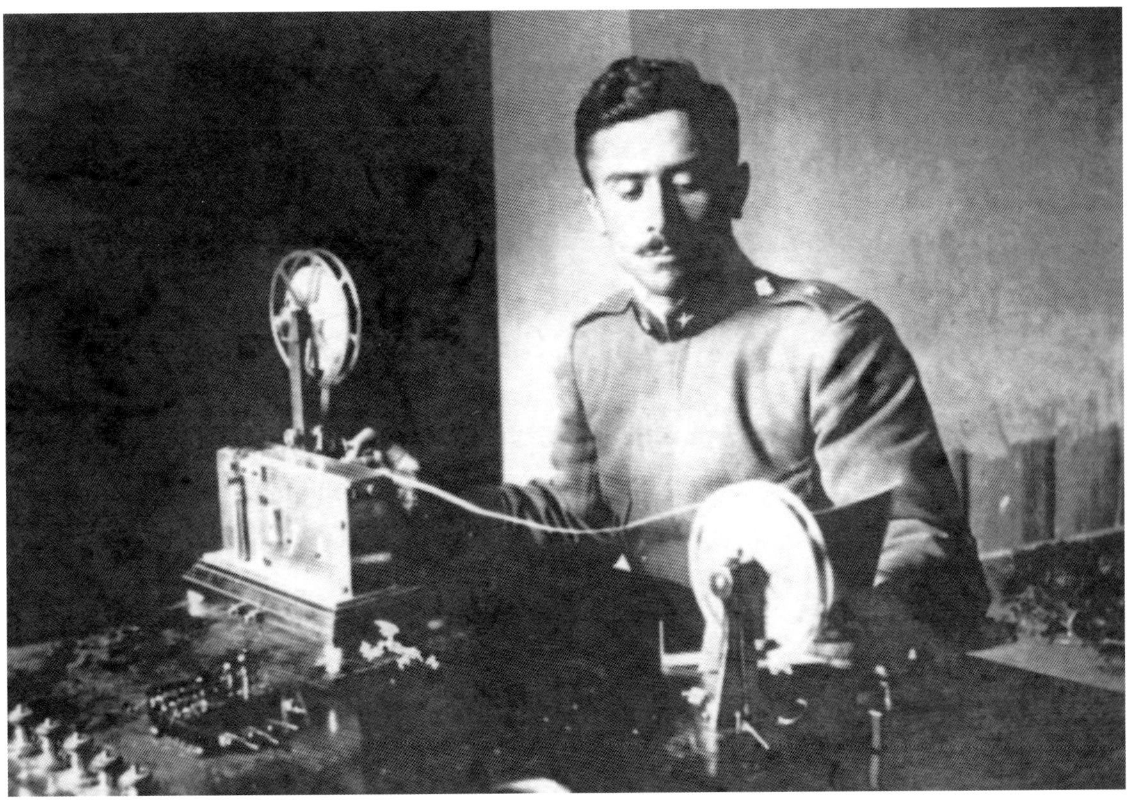

The mustached soldier (*soldato*) working at this table wears a gray green wool tunic (*Giacca*) with five pointed metal star (*Stellette*) insignia fastened to the collar.

This mustached switchboard operator wears a cotton tunic (*Giacca*) with gray green wool pants (*Pantaloni*) and puttees (*Fasce mollettiere*).

Twenty-four *soldati* (soldiers) armed with 6.5mm caliber Model 1891 Carcano bolt action rifles.

This group of soldiers poses for a photo clad in various cuts and styles of *grigioverde* (gray green) wool and cotton tunics.

Six *soldati* (soldiers) are resting on the grass wearing gray green wool uniforms. The soldier on the left has motorist insignia stitched to the sleeve of his tunic, and on his field cap.

The two soldiers seated on a bench wearing *grigioverde* (gray green) wool tunics, trousers, field caps, and puttees have removed their overcoats.

Eight *soldati* (soldiers) dressed in *grigioverde* (gray green) wool uniforms pause a photo while enjoying music and a drink.

The mustached officer (*Ufficiale*) relaxing on the ground wears a privately tailored gray green wool tunic (*Giacca*) with pleated pockets. He has belted his *giacca* with a brass buckle leather belt (*Cinturone*).

Two mustached soldiers clad in gray green tunics and trousers pose for a photo with their canine companion. This photo offers a glimpse of camp life during the Great War (*Grande Guerra*).

A group of weary soldiers clad in gray green wool pose for a photo with their equipment during a light snowfall.

These two mustached soldiers pose for a photo outside a tent offering a glimpse of camp life.

These four bivouacked soldiers pose for a photo while enjoying a drink and a meal.

Leaning on his bicycle, this soldier poses for a photo dressed in a gray green wool uniform with a dispatch pouch flung over his right shoulder. His comrade wears cotton fatigues and a gray green wool field cap.

This group of *soldati* (soldiers) clad in gray green wool uniforms and cotton fatigues poses for a photo while enjoying a drink from their canteens and a bite to each from their mess kits.

This unique photo displays a group of frontline troops clad in gray green wool uniforms and Model 1915 Adrian steel helmets relaxing after an action.

Standing guard outside his bunker during a light snowfall, this soldier poses for a photo wearing a gray green wool uniform and Model 1915 Adrian steel helmet. He is armed with a 6.5mm caliber Model 1891 Carcano bolt-action rifle.

A group of *soldati* (soldiers) clad in gray green wool uniforms pauses for a photo before securing their section. The sign bearing the number 15 indicates their section of the line they are to defend.

This unique photo was taken by a frontline soldier from inside his bunker.

The soldier wearing a *grigioverde* (gray green) wool uniform is standing in what appears to be an abandoned section of a trench line.

The soldier wearing a *grigioverde* (gray green) uniform staring into the air has placed his 6.5mm caliber Model 1891 bolt-rifle on snow-dusted rocks.

This soldier dressed in a gray green wool uniform and armed with a 6.5mm caliber Model 1891 bolt-action rifle appears to be one of the only soldiers guarding this particular trench line.

This group of *soldati* (soldiers) pose for a photo on a small bridge in a village near the front.

This soldier wearing a Model 1915 Adrian steel helmet and gray green wool tunic stares at church that was ravaged be shellfire.

This soldier in a *grigioverde* (gray green) wool uniform examines a church ravaged by shellfire.

Examining a chapel ravaged by shellfire.

This soldier, wearing a gray green wool Model 1915 field cap and overcoat, poses for a photo in a village near the front with his battle weary comrades in the background.

A candid photo of battle weary soldiers outfitted in *grigioverde* (gray green) wool field tunics and caps.

This grenadier poses for a photo dressed in a gray green wool uniform outside his barracks. The field cap of another comrade is visible over his right shoulder.

This group of soldiers poses for a photo outside of their bunker buried in snow. They are equipped with snow *occhiali*, or goggles.

Alpini in winter camouflage skiing.

This photo displays a crashed and burned Italian aircraft next to an abandoned Red Cross wagon.

Abandoned wagons, trucks, and fallen horses on the road to Udine. This photo is dated 4.11.17.

Abandoned wagons, trucks, and fallen horses on the road to Udine.

These Austro-Hungarian soldiers, with their horses and motorcycle, stand on a dirt road to Udine near captured Italian artillery pieces.

Austro-Hungarian soldiers standing on a dirt road to Udine near a captured Italian artillery piece.

A soldier dressed in a gray green wool uniform standing in snow covered mountains.

Barbed wire defenses in snow covered mountains.

Wood and barbed wire obstacles covered in snow.

Barbed wire entanglement in snow capped mountains.

Wood and barbed wire obstacles in mountainous terrain.

These six mustached soldiers are from the 69th Regiment, as the black thread numbers stitched on their *grigioverde* (gray green) wool *berretti* (field caps) with leather chin straps and visors indicate.

High ranking officers clad in gray green wool uniforms observing aircraft and enemy positions.

Chapter Twelve

Pioneers and Technical Units

(*Genio*)

This soldier clad in a gray green wool tunic and cap is from a technical unit attached to an aerodrome. He is equipped with a leather ammo bandolier.

This soldier wrapped in a gray green wool cloak (*Mantellina*) has technical/communication unit insignia stitched to his field cap (*berretto*). He is attached to a blimp/dirigible unit.

This soldier wears a gray green (*grigioverde*) wool tunic with a pen in his breast pocket, and a field cap bearing pioneer insignia.

This soldier wears a privately tailored pleated breast pocketed gray green wool field tunic (*Giacca*) with five pointed metal stars (*Stellette*) fastened to his collar, and a cap (*berretto*) with pioneer/engineer insignia stitched above the leather chinstrap and visor.

The soldier in this studio photo wears a gray green wool tunic with five pointed star collar insignia and cap bearing telegraph operator (*Telegrafista scelto*) insignia.

In this studio photo the mustached soldier wears a gray green (*grigioverde*) wool field tunic with decoration ribbon (*Nastrino*) and technical unit insignia stitched to his sleeve.

Holding his nickel plated Model 1888 saber (*Sciabola*) with his white gloved hands, this mustached soldier poses proudly for in this pre to early war vintage studio photo wearing a double-breasted black wool tunic with brass buttons and cap with gold stitched pioneer/engineer insignia.

Wrapped in a cloak (*Mantellina*), the soldier in this studio photo wears a privately tailored black wool field cap with gold stitched rank stripes and railroad pioneer insignia.

Leaning on a table, this soldier poses proudly for a studio photo wearing a gray green wool tunic (*Giacca*), trousers (*Pantaloni*), and puttees (*Mollettiere*). He has placed his field cap bearing pioneer insignia on top of his cloak (*Mantellina*).

This group of pioneers clad in gray green wool (*grigioverde*) uniforms poses proudly for a photo with their snow sculpture.

This group of pioneers/engineers poses proudly for a photo standing on a bridge and in pontoon boats.

This group of pioneers poses for a late war vintage photo clad in various models of gray green wool field tunics and caps.

Clad in cotton fatigues and gray green wool field caps with pioneer insignia, this group of pioneers poses for a photo in a wooded area.

Chapter Thirteen

POWs

Surrounded by his Austro-Hungarian captors, this dark haired Italian pilot poses relaxed and confident for a photo.

This Italian officer poses proudly for a photo with captured Austro-Hungarian prisoners dressed in *feldgrau* (field Gray).

This POW poses for a photo dressed in a gray green (*grigioverde*) wool field tunic (*Giacca*) with an identification number, and a cap (*Berretto*) with leather chinstrap and visor. This photo was taken in a prisoner of war camp on November 11, 1918.

Two *Alpini* dressed in gray green (*grigioverde*) wool uniforms pose for a photo by a barbed wire fence with Austro-Hungarian guards on the other side dressed in field gray (*feldgrau*) uniforms.

A group Italian prisoners of war relaxing on the ground clad in gray green wool uniforms.

Ten Italian POWs captured during a battle on the Isonzo Front.

This group of captured soldiers poses for a photo clad in gray green (*grigioverde*) wool uniforms and Model 1915 Adrian steel helmets. Austro-Hungarian soldiers often wore captured helmets, and sometimes added *FJI*—the initials of their Kaiser (Franz Joseph I).

Two Italian prisoners of war pose for a photo wearing gray green (*grigioverde*) wool uniforms with their Austro-Hungarian captors dressed in field gray (*feldgrau*).

Italian POWs clad in a variety of models of gray green uniforms pose for a group photo, which was most likely taken by their Austro-Hungarian captors.

This group of Italian prisoners of war pauses for a photo with their Austro-Hungarian captors while being marched down a mountain road.

A group of captured Italian soldiers clad in gray green wool uniforms and Model 1915 Adrian steel helmets being marched down a mountain by their Austro-Hungarian captors.

Many of the Austro-Hungarian soldiers in this group photo wear captured Italian uniforms. Two of these soldiers wear captured gray green (*grigioverde*) wool field caps.

Italian and Czarist Russian prisoners of war, April 1916.

A group of Italian POWs clad in gray green wool uniforms resting on the ground in a town near the front lines.

Seated on the ground, this group of Italian prisoners of war pose for a photo with their Austro-Hungarian captor wearing a variety of gray green (*grigioverde*) wool field tunics and caps.

This group of Italian POWs in Laibach were captured on the Isonzo front.

Captured on the Isonzo front, and later taken to Laibach, this group of Italian prisoners of war marches past a photographer wearing their gray green wool field tunics and caps. The number 30 on their cap indicates their unit.

Italian POWs (*Kriegsgefangenen*) carrying water.

Two Austro-Hungarian soldiers helping a wounded Italian *Kriegsgefangener*, or prisoner of war.

Chapter Fourteen

Libyan and Colonial Campaigns

Five *soldati* (soldiers) wearing wool tunics, trousers, and puttees pose for a photo with a child and canine companions in this studio photo taken in Tripoli, Libya.

Italian officers, and the local population in Libya.

Indigenous cavalry and Italian infantry pose for a photo at an outpost. The reverse of this photo reads in Italian "Raising our flag on a '*Marabutto*' near Cirene."

Italian officers mingling with the local population in Libya.

Indigenous and Italian cavalry and infantry.

Indigenous infantry poses proudly for a photo with Italian soldiers on a road. The reverse of this photo reads in Italian *"At Cheren, waiting for His Excellence the Governor - January 21, 1914."*

Two of the *soldati* (soldiers) in this photo taken in Libya wear cotton covered pith helmets with unit insignia fastened to the front. The other three *soldati* wear wool field caps with leather visors fashioned after the Model 1909.

This soldier, wearing a wool tunic (*Giacca*) and cap (*Berretto*), poses proudly for a photo with his camel and local guide.

Soldati (soldiers) departing for Tripoli.

An encampment in Libya.

On board the ship *Rio Amazonas* en route to Tolmetta Harbor. December 30, 1913.

An exhibition of Abyssinian *Ascari*.

The indigenous cavalryman mounted on his horse wears a white cotton uniform with a sash and wool fez. The Italian cavalry officer holding the reigns of his horse wears a privately tailored tunic and white field cap with rank stripes and unit insignia.

Mounted on a white horse, this mustached cavalry officer poses proudly for a photo wearing a privately tailored pleated breast pocketed khaki tunic. He holds a baton in his right hand.

This is a souvenir photo taken at the home of His Royal Highness Duca Delle Puglie Torino.

The mustached officer in this studio photo with his hands on his saber (*Sciabola*) poses confidently wearing a khaki pith helmet and privately tailored uniform. This photo was taken in a studio in Naples (*Napoli*) Italy.

The goateed soldier wears a cotton tunic (*Giacca*) with five pointed star (*Stellette*) insignia fastened to the collar. Cotton uniforms, such as the one this soldier has on, were worn by troops serving in warm climates.

Chapter Fifteen

Pre to Early War

Italian soldiers in service in the Far East.

The mustached soldier in this pre to early war vintage photo wears a dark colored wool tunic (*Giacca*) with brass buttons and five pointed star (*Stellette*) metal collar insignia fastened to his collar. The number 52 on his brass badge (*Fregio*) fastened to his field cap indicates his unit.

Holding the handles of his bicycle, this soldier poses for a photo outside of his barracks wearing a cotton tunic with rank chevrons and braids stitched to his sleeves. His field cap is made of dark colored wool, and has a leather visor and chinstrap.

Seven soldiers in full battle dress pose for a pre to early war vintage photo on a mountainside.

This group of *soldati* (soldiers) wearing dark wool tunics and light colored cotton fatigues poses for a pre to early war vintage photo taken in their camp.

In this pre to early war vintage cabinet portrait taken in Salerno, Italy, the mustached artillery officer wears a dark colored wool double-breasted tunic and cap with gold stitched insignia.

The mustached soldier in this cabinet portrait wears a double-breasted wool tunic with brass buttons. The gold stitched crown and number 50 on his dark color wool cap (*berretto*) indicate his unit.

The mustached artillerist wrapped in a cloak in this pre to early war vintage cabinet portrait taken in Padova, Italy, wears a dark colored wool cap (*Berretto*) bearing crossed cannon insignia. He is a member of the Royal Italian Navy.

The mustached infantry officer in this pre to early war vintage cabinet portrait has three medals fastened to the chest of his double-breasted wool tunic. His field cap (*Berretto*) appears to have been privately purchased, instead of being issued from a depot.

This mustached soldier wears a high collared single breasted wool tunic with technical unit insignia stitched to his sleeve.

Holding his saber (Sciabola) with both hands, this *Ardito* poses proudly for a photo clad in a pre to early war vintage dark colored wool tunic with *Arditi* unit insignia stitched to his sleeve.

The officer in this studio photo wears a dark colored wool dolman with a decoration ribbon. He has five pointed star insignia fastened to his shoulder boards and collar.

Seated on a wicker bench, these two *soldati* (soldiers) pose for a photo with their canine friend wearing black wool tunics with brass buttons.

Three *soldati* (soldiers) in full battle dress, armed with 6.5mm caliber Model 1891 Carcano bolt action rifles with bayonets.

With his hand resting near his field cap (*Berretto*), this soldier poses proudly, wearing a dark colored wool tunic (*Giacca*) with brass buttons.

Holding a baton in his right hand and his leather gloves in his left, this mustached soldiers poses confidently in this pre to early war vintage studio photo wearing a black dolman with a decoration ribbon, and five pointed star (*Stellette*) metal collar insignia fastened to his collar.

The soldier in this pre to early war vintage cabinet portrait wears a single breasted wool tunic with brass buttons and shoulder boards (*Spalline*) bearing his unit insignia.

The mustached soldier seated in this studio photo wears a single breasted black tunic with brass buttons. He wears a gray green (*grigioverde*) wool field cap (*Berretto*) with the number 73 stitched above the leather chinstrap of the cap.

Three mustached officers wearing privately tailored wool tunics pose proudly for a photo armed with Model 1888 sabers.

In this pre to early war vintage cabinet portrait, a soldier poses proudly wearing a single breasted black wool tunic with brass buttons and five pointed star collar insignia. He has metal insignia bearing the number 88 fastened to his black wool field cap (*Berretto*).

Two mustached *soldati* (soldiers) wearing black wool uniforms pose proudly for a studio photo with the barrel of their artillery piece.

In this pre to early war vintage studio photo, a mustached soldier wearing a black wool tunic with brass buttons rests his hand on a pedestal where he has placed his field cap.

The soldier in this pre to early war studio photo wears a black wool overcoat with pads on the ends of his shoulders to keep his rifle sling from slipping off. He has placed his cap (*Berretto*) bearing metal unit insignia on a pedestal.

This soldier wears a black wool tunic with brass buttons and gray green (*grigioverde*) wool trousers. He has placed his *grigioverde* cloak (*Mantellina*) and field cap (*Berretto*) on an intricately carved chair.

Leaning on an ornately carved pedestal, this mustached soldier poses for a pre to early war vintage studio photo wearing a black wool tunic with brass buttons and five pointed star (*Stellette*) collar insignia. He is armed with a Vetterli bayonet.

In this pre to early war vintage studio photo, a soldier poses proudly wearing a single breasted black wool tunic and holding his saber. His black wool cap (*Berretto*) bears metal crossed cannon insignia, indicating he is an artillerist.

Although appearing to be a pre to early war vintage black wool cap and tunic, this is actually the dress tunic of the *Carabinieri* (Gendarme/Military Police). Note that this uniform was not worn on the front lines.

This mustached soldier wears a double-breasted black wool tunic and cap. His cap, as well as his collar insignia, indicates he is *Cavalleria*, or cavalry.

The mustached soldier holding his gloves in this pre to early war studio wears a double-breasted gala dress uniform with a medal.

With his right hand resting on a pedestal, and his left hand grasping his saber with sword knot, this mustached soldier poses for a pre to early war photo wearing a double-breasted black wool tunic and trousers.

Holding the handles of their bicycles, and dressed in what appear to be pre to early war dark colored wool uniforms, two *Carabinieri* (Gendarme/ Military Police) pose proudly for a photo. The black wool uniform of the *Carabinieri* was only worn behind the frontlines, which is most likely where this photo was taken.

This soldier poses proudly for a pre to early war vintage studio photo wearing a double-breasted gala tunic with five pointed star insignia fasted to his collar.

These two *Carabinieri* (Gendarme/Military Police) pose for a pre to early war vintage studio photo wearing their traditional black wool uniforms.

The soldier in this studio photo wears a black wool dolman with five pointed star (*Stellette*) insignia fastened to his collar and shoulder straps (*Spalline*).

The mustached cavalryman in this studio portrait wears a black wool tunic and overcoat with fur collar. He has five pointed star collar insignia fastened to the collars of his tunic and overcoat.

This soldier wears a black wool tunic with brass buttons and five pointed star insignia fastened to his collar. In addition, he has infantry insignia fastened to his black wool field cap (*Berretto*).

Leaning on a pedestal, this mustached soldier poses proudly for photo wearing a black wool tunic with brass buttons and five pointed star collar insignia. His field cap (*Berretto*) bears crossed cannon insignia, indicating he is in an artillery unit. He is armed with a Vetterli bayonet.

In this pre to early war vintage studio photo, a soldier poses proudly for a photo wearing a dark colored wool tunic and fez with a tassel. This style of dress was favored by elite troops, such as the *Bersaglieri*.

Six *soldati* (soldiers) from the 39th Regiment pose for a photo outside of their tent clad in dark colored wool and light cotton tunics. White cotton covers often were worn over wool field caps (*Berretti*) during maneuvers.

The mustached artillery officer in this pre to early war vintage cabinet portrait wears a double-breasted dark colored wool tunic and cap (*Berretto*) with rank stripes and crossed cannon insignia.

These *soldati* (soldiers) pose for a group photo in the Italian countryside clad in a variety of tunics and caps.

Soldati (soldiers) armed with 6.5mm caliber Model 1891 Carcano bolt action rifles on the march.

The artillerist in this pre to early war vintage cabinet portrait wears a single-breasted black wool tunic with five pointed star collar insignia, and a plumed cap with crossed cannon insignia. He holds a pair of white gloves in his right hand and a saber in his left.

Three artillerists pose proudly for a studio photo dressed in single-breasted black wool tunics with brass buttons and five pointed star insignia fastened to their collars.

Two mustached *soldati* (soldiers) wearing black wool uniforms pose for a photo with three of their companions dressed in civilian clothing in this pre to early war vintage photo.

These soldiers wear a pre to early war style of tunics and riding britches. The style headdress each one is wearing was referred to a *cappello a visera a due punte* (two-pointed forage/tent cap with a visor).

Nine *soldati* (soldiers) clad in cotton uniforms pose for a group photo while enjoying food and drink. Cotton uniforms were often preferred over wool because they could be laundered more easily.

Superimposed on this *Made in Austria* French Christmas card depicting an angel watching over the Virgin Mary and the infant Jesus is a photo of a young Italian military musician dressed in a double-breasted tunic with cordage.

This mustached soldier poses confidently wearing a single breasted black wool tunic with brass buttons and rank chevrons stitched to his sleeves.

In this cabinet portrait taken in Venice (*Venezia*), Italy, a mustached soldier from a medical unit poses proudly wearing a black wool dolman and cap (*Berretto*).

These *soldati* (soldiers) pose for a pre to early war vintage group photo clad in various models of tunics and headdresses.

Chapter Sixteen

Steel Helmets

This soldier poses proudly for a late war vintage studio photo wearing an Italian manufactured Model 1916 steel helmet with infantry insignia. The design of Model 1916 (*Modello 1916*) was based on the French manufactured Model 1915 Adrian helmet. Although almost identical to each other in design, there remain subtle variations in shape and construction.

In this unique photo, three brave Italian *soldati* (soldiers) wearing gray green (*grigioverde*) wool tunics and Austro-Hungarian manufactured Berndorfer helmets pose for a photo in front of a sandbagged position.

This group of *soldati* (soldiers), wearing both Italian manufactured Model 1916 and French manufactured Model 1915 Adrian steel helmets, pauses for a photo before engaging advancing Austro-Hungarian forces. The soldier preparing to throw a hand grenade has chosen to wear a gray green wool Model 1909 field cap.

A group of soldiers wearing Italian manufactured Model 1916 and French manufactured Model 1915 Adrian steel helmets painted gray green (*grigioverde*) at work in rock covered terrain. Some of these soldiers have chosen to wear *grigioverde* wool field caps (*berretti*).

This group of *soldati* (soldiers) poses for photo in full battle dress armed with 6.5mm caliber M1891 Carcano bolt action rifles. All appear to be wearing Italian manufactured Model 1916 steel helmets, which are painted gray green (*grigioverde*).

This smiling soldier wears an Italian manufactured Model 1916 steel helmet. In addition, he is equipped with a bolt-action rifle, leather Model 1907 ammo pouches (*Giberna*), a lanyard attached to a holstered side arm, bayonet with frog, and a wool covered canteen.

Relaxing in a farmer's field, four soldiers pose for a photo wearing gray green wool uniforms. The soldier on the left is armed with a Model 1889 revolver, and the reclining soldier on the right is equipped with a Polivalente gas mask. They have removed their Italian manufactured Model 1916 steel helmets and wool field caps.

A group of *soldati* (soldiers) wearing Italian manufactured Model 1916 steel helmets and gray green wool uniforms gather around an officer on a platform giving a speech.

This group of soldiers wearing Italian manufactured Model 1916 steel helmets and gray green (*grigioverde*) wool field caps poses for a photo with some of the locals from a town near the front. Many are armed with 6.5mm caliber Model 1891 Carcano bolt-action rifles.

A group of *soldati* (soldiers) poses for a photo outside of a building wearing Italian manufactured Model 1916 steel helmets and gray green wool uniforms. Many are equipped with leather ammo bandoliers.

Standing on rocky terrain near barbed wire entanglements with a walking stick, a soldier poses wearing an Italian manufactured Model 1916 steel helmet and gray green wool tunic, trousers, and puttees. He is equipped with a foreign manufactured gas mask, which he wears around his neck.

Standing in brass shell casings, this soldier poses for a photo wearing Italian manufactured Model 1916 steel helmet (*Elmo italiano Modello 1916*) with cloth cover (*Telino*) and gray green wool uniform. He wears a foreign manufactured gas mask around his neck.

The soldier with his back turned to the camera conversing with three officers wears an Italian manufactured Model 1916 steel helmet with cloth cover (*Telino*). Cloth covers protected not only the finish, but also camouflaged the helmet.

Battle weary *soldati* (soldiers) clad in gray green wool uniforms and Italian manufactured Model 1916 steel helmets pause for a photo on the frontlines during a light snowfall.

Four soldiers pose for a photo on the front wearing Italian manufactured Model 1916 steel helmets and wool field caps (*Berretti*).

Three *soldati* (soldiers) wearing gray green (*grigioverde*) wool uniforms pose for a photo near a battle damaged dwelling. Two of these three *soldati* wear Italian manufactured Model 1916 steel helmets with cloth covers.

Holding a cigarette between the fingers of his left hand, this soldier poses for a photo wearing a gray green wool uniform and Italian manufactured Model 1916 steel helmet.

Two *soldati* (soldiers) wearing gray green wool uniforms and Italian manufactured Model 1916 steel helmets pose for a late war vintage photo.

These grenadiers (*granatieri*) pose for a photo in a town near the front wearing Italian manufactured Model 1916 steel helmets with cloth covers bearing their unit insignia.

This soldier bivouacked in a town near the front poses for a photo holding his walking stick and wearing a French manufactured Model 1915 Adrian steel helmet. In addition, he is equipped with a Polivalente gas mask (*la maschera*).

Twenty-two soldiers (*soldati*) wearing Model 1909 gray green (*grigioverde*) wool field caps (*Berretti*) and Italian manufactured Model 1916 steel helmets pose for a group photo in rocky terrain near the front lines, 1918.

Chapter Seventeen

Air Service

This aviator dressed in a gray green wool field cap and cotton flight suit poses for a photo staring into a clear sky. He is seated in the cockpit of a Nieuport 10, with roundels in the national colors painted on the fuselage. The Nieuport 10 was a French design that was licensed to be manufactured in Italy.

Pilot and ground crew clad in gray green wool uniforms prepare their French manufactured Farman F.50 bomber before a flight over the front.

Pilots and ground crew dressed in cotton work fatigues pose for a group photo inside their barracks with a wood propeller in the center.

This pilot and ground crew pose for a photo with their Caproni Ca 1214 bomber. Arrows indicate where the "*bombe*" are located on the plane.

Ground crewmen and pilots from a *Squadriglia* (Squadron) *Caproni* pose for a photo wearing gray green (*grigioverde*) wool uniforms.

Pilot and ground crew pose for a photo with their Nieuport 10 parked in a grassy field. This Nieuport 10, with roundels in the national colors painted on the fuselage, was a French design licensed to be manufactured in Italy.

This pilot wearing a gray green wool tunic pauses for a photo before climbing into the cockpit of his Hanriot Hd 1.

Pilot and ground crew pose for a photo with their canine companion outside of an aircraft hangar for the 31st Squadron (*Squadriglia*) in Verona, Italy, October 1916.

Dressed in gray green wool field tunics and caps, this pilot and ground crew pose for a photo with their Henri Farman H.F. 27 parked outside a hangar.

This aviator poses proudly wearing a gray green (*grigioverde*) wool tunic and field cap with leather visor and chinstrap. He has winged propeller insignia stitched to the sleeve of his tunic.

Pilot and ground crew pose for a photo with their Hanriot Hd. 1 parked in a grassy field.

Clad in cotton work fatigues and a dark colored wool cap, this pilot or ground crew member poses for a photo with his Hanriot Hd. 1.

These two soldiers dressed in gray green wool tunics, trousers, and puttees pose proudly for a photo with a Hanriot Hd. 1.

In this 1917 vintage photo a pilot and ground crew clad in gray green wool uniforms pose with their biplane.

Pilots and ground crew pose for a photo with their Farman 1914 or Maurice Farman M.F. 11 parked outside a hangar covered with canvas tarps.

Dressed in a variety of tunics and field caps, these pilots and ground crew from a Farman squadron pose for a group photo.

Eleven ground crewmen and pilots wearing gray green wool tunics and cotton fatigues pose for a photo with their biplane.

Soldiers and children look in awe at the wreckage of an Austro-Hungarian aircraft.

Examining the wreckage of an aircraft.

Soldati (soldiers) clad in gray green (grigioverde) wool uniforms and civilians gathered around a Deperdussin TT.

This group of *soldati* (soldiers), wearing various models of gray green (*grigioverde*) wool tunics and field caps, pause for a photo while examining wreckage.

Two officers in gray green wool tunics and field caps examine the wreckage of an aircraft.

A group of *soldati* (soldiers) examine the wreckage of an Austro-Hungarian aircraft.

Soldati (soldiers) examine an aircraft that crashed and burned.

Examining the wreckage of an aircraft.

A group of *soldati* (soldiers) examine the crash site of an overturned Austro-Hungarian aircraft.

Examining the wreckage, Verona, Italy, 1916.

Soldati (soldiers) clad in gray green wool and cotton tunics examining a captured Austro-Hungarian aircraft.

Pilots and ground crew pose for a photo with their floatplane parked outside a hangar.

The pilot wearing a leather jacket has removed his Roold flight helmet to pose for a photo before taking off in his Blériot 11.

This crew poses for a photo with their flying boat on the Adriatic.

Pilot, crew, and local civilians pose for a photo before take off.

A group of *soldati* (soldiers) examining the wreckage of an Austro-Hungarian aircraft.

This pilot, holding his flight helmet, wears a leather jacket over his gray green wool tunic and poses for a photo with his Morane-Saulnier before take-off.

Looking at his notebook, this aviator poses for a photo wearing a privately tailored, pleated pocketed gray green (*grigioverde*) wool tunic (*Giacca*) with gold stitched aviator insignia on his sleeve.

These pilots and ground crewman pose for a photo while enjoying a drink.

Clad in a fur lined leather flight suit, this mustached second lieutenant poses for a photo on the day of his first take-off.

Montecchio, 1918. This photo is captioned in Italian "My chickens of Aviatik and SAML/2."

Clad in gray green wool uniforms and Roold flight helmets, this group of pilots and ground crew pose for a photo with their biplane. This photo is captioned in Italian "My Chickens!"

This photo is captioned in Italian, "The one who failed in Montecchio Training School! S.V.A.-9."

A group of flight school engineers clad in gray green wool uniforms pose proudly with their S.V.A. Montecchio Est.

Montecchio Est. S.V.A.

A shot of the airfield at 100 meters.

Flying over the aircraft hangars at 100 meters.

Chapter Eighteen

Navy/Marine

An Italian submarine and her crew on the Adriatic, 1916.

R.N. Compania and her crew on the Adriatic.

A crew and their naval cannon on the Mediterranean.

A coastal patrol boat and her crew on the Adriatic.

This group of sailors poses for a photo on the docks wearing a variety of tunics and caps.

Naval officers dressed in white uniforms pose for a photo with soldiers from other branches of the armed forces.

Forty-five naval officers and other ranks pose for a group clad in dark colored wool tunics and overcoats. Many have been decorated and have rank chevrons stitched to their sleeves.

This naval landing party poses for a group photo dressed in gray green (*grigioverde*) wool uniforms.

Naval officers and their children, 1916.

The naval marine in this studio photo is from San Marco, as the tally on his gray green (*grigioverde*) wool cap indicates.

The sailor seated in the studio photo dressed in white is from a torpedo boat, as the tally on his cap and his sleeve insignia indicates.

These three soldiers wearing dark colored wool caps with tallies from three different ships pose proudly for a pre to early war vintage studio photo.

Chapter Nineteen

Special Units and Volunteers

Dressed in a treated cloth suit and hood for protection, this soldier prepares to demonstrate a flamethrower, or *lancia-fiamme*.

The soldier dressed in the treated cloth suit in this photo is from a flamethrower unit.

Officers and other ranks dress in gray green wool uniforms preparing to review a flamethrower unit.

A flamethrower unit preparing to ignite.

Flamethrower unit in action.

Firing a flamethrower (*lanciafiamme*) from a foxhole.

This photo displays results from firing a flamethrower (*lanciafiamme*).

In this photo the flamethrower unit is firing into black clouds of smoke on a burning field.

The results of firing a flamethrower (*lanciafiamme*).

This soldier, in a gray green (*grigioverde*) wool uniform, poses for a photo in a burning field with black clouds of smoke. The field was set afire by a flamethrower (*lanciafiamme*) unit.

Two Americans from an ambulance unit peeling potatoes outside of a villa in Northern Italy.

The American standing near barbed wire entanglements loading his rifle is from an ambulance unit that was sent to Italy to help the Italians with their wounded during the First World War.

This American from an ambulance unit pauses for a photo before patching tires for ambulances.

Ambulances from an American medical unit parked in a courtyard in Northern Italy.

Two Americans from a medical unit wearing Brodie helmets, and equipped with U.S. manufactured gasmasks pause for a photo next to barbed wire entanglements near the front with their motorcycle from the Medical Department of the U.S. Army.

Italian soldiers dressed in gray green (*grigioverde*) wool uniforms marching down a road in Northern Italy. This photo was taken from the front seat of an ambulance from an American volunteer medical unit.

Two American (Doughboys) soldiers pose for a photo in Lido. Lido is an island in the Adriatic located between the Gulf of Venice and the Lagoon of Venice.

Three American soldiers seated on a bench outside a hospital in Gorizia, Italy.

This American soldier poses for a photo in some ancient ruins in Gorizia, Italy.

With his tunic flung over his shoulder and his left hand in his pocket, this American soldier poses for a photo in Gorizia, Italy.

An American soldier seated in wreckage in Gorizia, Italy.

An American soldier examining artillery rounds in wood crates with rope handles. Gorizia, Italy.

Two American soldiers and Italian civilians pose for a photo before boarding a horse-drawn streetcar. Gorizia, Italy.

Five American soldiers pose for a photo in a lightly wooded are outside a fortress in Northern Italy. Two of these five soldiers are using entrenching tools.

An American driver pauses for a photo with his spoke wheel truck parked on a road with other vehicles headed to the front lines.

Fourteen *soldati* (soldiers) pose for a group photo clad in various models of field tunics and caps armed with bolt-action rifles and bayonets. The four *soldati* seated on the ground are enjoying a meal and a drink from their mess kits and Model 1907 wooden canteens.

Fourteen *soldati* (soldiers) with a bicycle pose for a group photo dressed in various models of field tunics and caps.

Eleven Italian soldiers in gray green wool uniforms, and armed with Austro-Hungarian manufactured M95 Gewehrs with bayonets. The sign in the center, as well as their collar and cap insignia, are characteristic of the Czech Legion.

With his left hand resting on his Model 1891 bayonet, this *Alpino* poses proudly for a studio photo wearing a privately tailored gray green (*grigioverde*) wool tunic with Czech Legion insignia stitched to his sleeve.

The Italian soldier in this cabinet portrait taken in Pilsen (PlzeH) wears a gray green wool tunic and cap with Czech Legion insignia.

Six Alpini pose proudly for a photo wearing gray green (*grigioverde*) wool tunics with Czech Legion insignia and armed with trench knives.

Chapter Twenty

Late to Post War

In this late to post war vintage photo two *soldati* (soldiers) wearing privately tailored gray green (*grigioverde*) wool tunics pose proudly with their motorcycle with sidecar.

Four *soldati* (soldiers) wearing gray green wool uniforms pose for this late to post war vintage photo in the entry of their barracks with a motorcycle with sidecar.

In this late to post war vintage photo, the two cavalrymen resting on the ground wear open collar tunics with black neckties.

This artillerist poses proudly for a late to post war vintage photo with his heavy cannon. He is armed with a 6.5mm caliber Model 1891 Carcano bolt-action rifle and bayonet.

A group of *soldati* (soldiers) enjoying a meal and a drink pause for a late to post war vintage photo.

The infantryman in this late to post war vintage studio photo wears a privately tailored pleated pocketed gray green (*grigioverde*) wool tunic with five pointed star insignia on his collar and shoulder boards.

In this late to post war vintage photo seven artillerists clad in gray green wool uniforms pose for a photo with their field cannon.

The officer in this late to post war vintage photo wears a privately tailored gray green wool tunic with five pointed star insignia on his cuffs, and *Arditi* unit insignia stitched to his sleeve.

Soldati (soldiers) dressed in gray green wool and white cotton tunics pose for a photo with their families.

The officer posing with a child in this late to post war vintage studio photo wears a privately tailored tunic with decoration bar stitched above his left breast pocket, and five pointed star insignia stitched to his collar and cuffs. He holds his saber with his left hand.

Six decorated *soldati* (soldiers) wearing various styles of field tunics and caps pose for a late to post war vintage photo.

Holding his saber in his white gloved hand, this decorated officer wearing a privately tailored gray green (*grigioverde*) wool tunic poses proudly for a photo with his bride in this late to post war vintage studio photo.

This mustached soldier poses proudly for a photo wearing a gray green wool tunic, pair of pants, and puttees.

Holding a pair of white gloves in his right hand, this infantryman poses for a late to post war studio photo wearing a privately tailored, pleated pocketed gray green wool tunic with brass buttons and five pointed star collar insignia.

This infantryman holding a pair of white gloves in his left hand wears a privately tailored gray green (grigioverde) wool tunic and baggy trousers. The vase on the table holding a bouquet of flowers is a brass artillery shell turned into trench art.

The soldier in this oval shaped studio portrait on this decorative patriotic postcard wears a gray green wool field tunic and cap. SPQR stands for *senatus populusque Romanus*, or Senate and people of Rome.

A decorated artillery officer in parade dress poses for a late to post war vintage photo with his female companion.

The mustached veteran officer in this oval shaped studio photo wears a pre to early war style black wool field cap, and has his medals and decorations stitched to his coat.

The mustached officer holding his saber in this late to post war vintage studio photo wears a privately tailored pleated pocketed gray green (*grigioverde*) wool tunic with gold stitched rank chevrons on his cuffs.

Chapter Twenty-One

Generals and Other High Ranking Officials

The mustached soldier in this photo documenting a presentation ceremony is having a medal of valor placed above the left breast pocket of his gray green wool tunic.

Allied officers and public dignitaries at a presentation ceremony.

Conversing before a presentation ceremony, 1918.

Generals, officers, and public officials at a presentation ceremony, 1918.

Officers dressed in privately tailored gray green wool uniforms and public dignitaries awaiting a presentation ceremony.

Allied officers and Red Cross nurses, 1918.

Awaiting a presentation ceremony, 1918.

Decorated members of the General Staff pose for a group photo wearing a variety of headdresses and tunics.

High ranking officers from various branches of the Italian and French armed forces.

General Staff (*Stato Maggiore*), 1918.

General Staff (*Stato Maggiore*), 1917.

Inspecting a barracks facility, 1917.

Seven members of the General Staff (*Stato Maggiore*) pose for a photo wearing various styles of privately tailored gray green (*grigioverde*) wool uniforms, 1918.

The mustached General in this shadowy studio photo wears a privately purchased gray green wool field cap with General Staff insignia, and an overcoat with a heavy fur collar.

In addition to having been awarded Military medals, this *Tenente General in commando di Corpo D Armata* also is decorated with civil and Vatican orders and medals, as well.

Color Gallery

Model 1909 gray green (*grigioverde*) wool field cap (*berretto*) with leather visor and railroad engineer insignia.

Depot issued Model 1909 gray green (*grigioverde*) wool field cap (*berretto*) with leather visor and stitched 2nd Regiment insignia.

Privately purchased gray green (*grigioverde*) wool field cap (*berretto*) with leather visor and gold stitched artillerist insignia.

Model 1915 gray green (*grigioverde*) wool field cap (*cupolino/scodellino*) with leather visor and medical unit insignia.

Wool felt *Alpini cappello* with leather sweat band and cloth lining. This *cappello* was worn by an *Alpini Aspirante* killed in action October 16, 1915, on Monte Nodice, Alto Garda zone.

Model 1910 gray green (*grigioverde*) felt *Alpini cappello* for a lieutenant in the 4th Alpini Regiment. The insignia and rank chevron are made of gray green wool silk.

Model 1910 gray green (*grigioverde*) felt *Alpini cappello* made of burlap with depot markings.

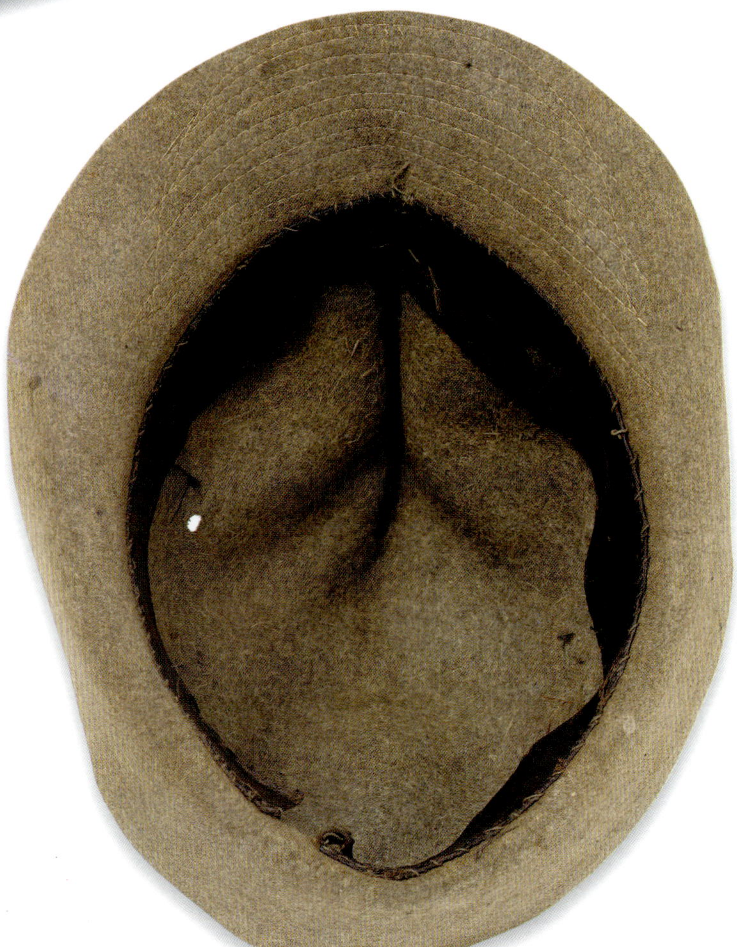

Enlisted rank gray green (*grigioverde*) wool felt *Alpini cappello* with leather sweatband.

Late to post war style black felt *Bersaglieri moretto* with leather chin strap and sweatband.

Black wool field cap (*berretto*) with leather visor and gold stitched rank and unit insignia.

Black wool field cap (*berretto*) with leather visor and machinegun unit insignia in original box.

Above and following: Italian manufactured aviator/pilot helmet made of cork and oilcloth with framed piece of wood from an Austro-Hungarian manufactured plane which was shot down by the owner of this helmet in 1918 over Albania

Hinten.
St. B.
K308

Front, rear, side and interior views of a helmet for Dragoons (*Dragoni*) with carrying case and gray green (*grigioverde*) wool cover. This model of helmet was reserved for *Dragoni* in Nizza, Piemont Reale, Savoia, and Genova regiments.

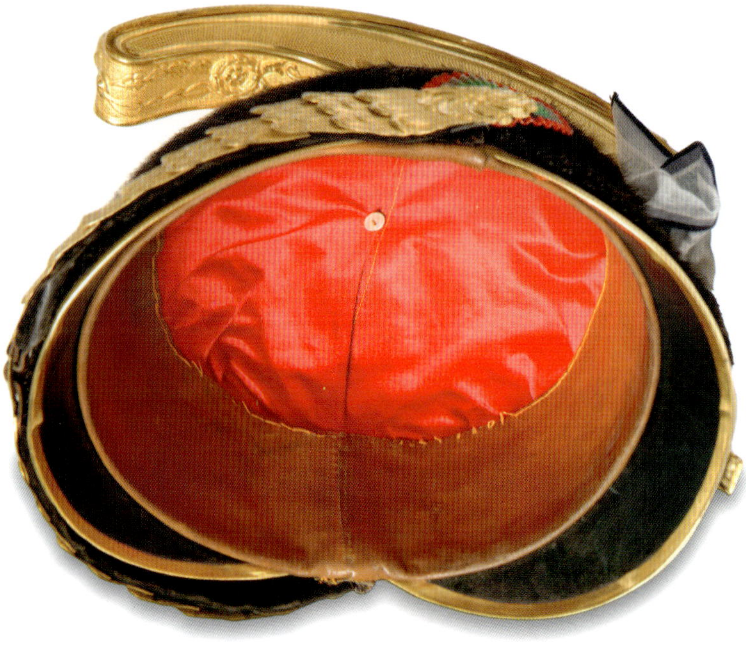

Farina Helmet (*Elmo Farina*) with leather chinstrap and factory stamp. Stamp reads "IL TAGLIA ING.F.FARINA-VIA RUFFINI 10 MILANO".

Farina Helmet (*Elmo Farina*) with leather chinstrap. Referred to often as the high/tall model.

Farina Helmet (*Elmo Farina*) with ventilation between the skull and front plate. This helmet was often referred to as the low model.

Interior and exterior views of a Model 1915 Adrian helmet with painted 39th Artillery Regiment insignia.

Model 1915 Adrian helmet with gray green (*grigioverde*) wool cover and stitched artillery unit insignia.

Model 1915 Adrian steel helmet with leather chinstrap and *Arditi* unit insignia.

Model 1915 Adrian steel helmet with *Alpini* unit insignia. This helmet was found in a glacier.

Model 1915 Adrian steel helmet with *piumetto* (plume) holder painted in the late to post war period.

Austro-Hungarian manufactured Berndorfer helmet of a forward observer/sentinel with battle damage. This helmet was recovered in the early 1990s on the Presena glacier in the Adamello-Presanella mountain region.

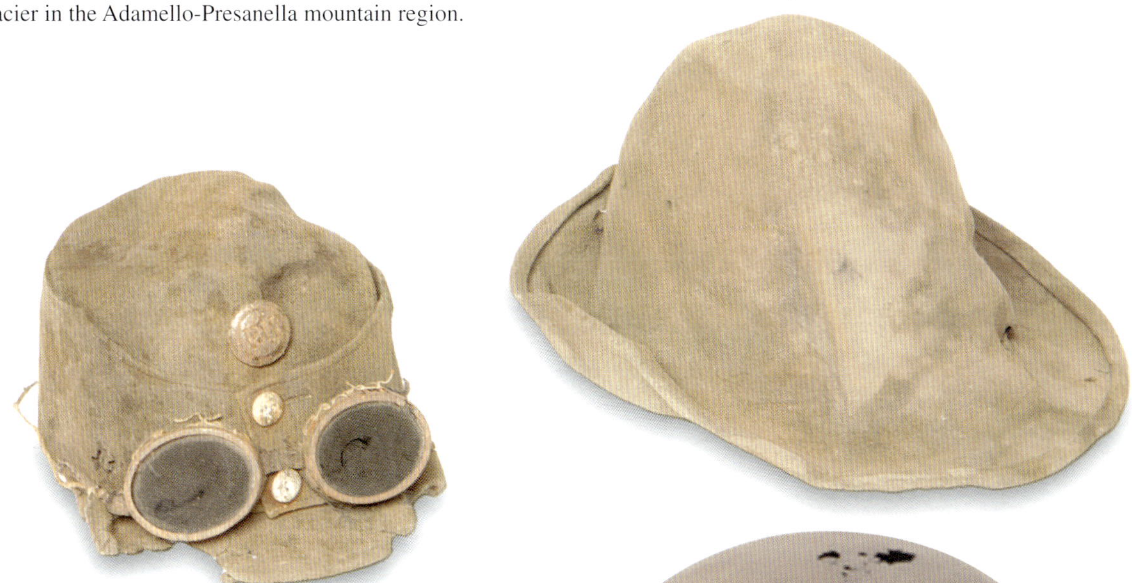

Austro-Hungarian manufactured field cap (*feldkappe*) and *Alpini cappello* found in the Adamello glacier during the late 1990s.

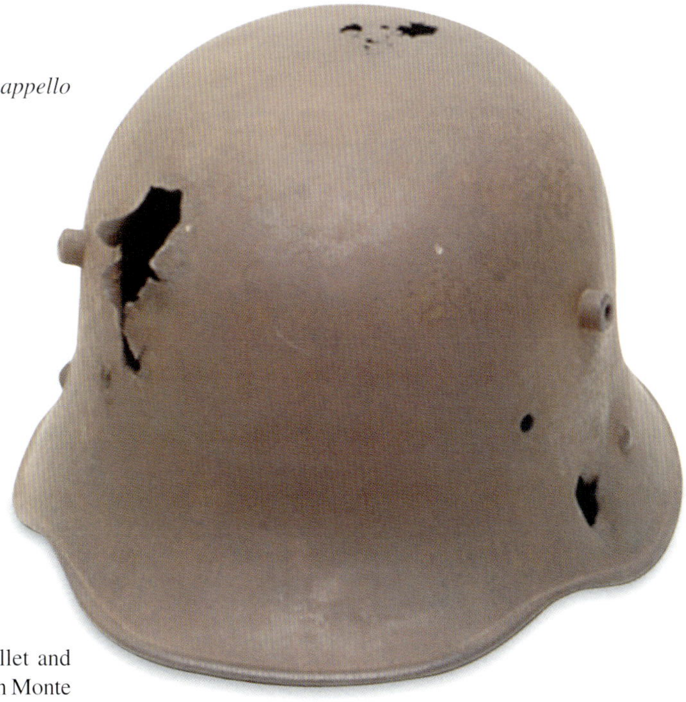

Austro-Hungarian manufactured Model 1917 *Stahlhelm* with bullet and shrapnel damage. This helmet was found during the interwar years on Monte Grappa.

Farina Helmet (*Elmo Farina*) with bullet and shrapnel damage. This helmet was recovered in the Carso mountains.

Below: Model 1915 Adrian steel helmet with Bersaglieri insignia and machinegun bullet and shrapnel damage. This helmet was recovered from a battlefield.

Model 1909 gray green (*grigioverde*) wool tunic from a soldier who served in the Bisagno Brigade (209th,210th Infantry Regiments) The stamp on the inner lining reads "COMMISSIONE PROVINCIALE PER INDUMENTI MILITARI DI LIVORNO".

Front and rear views of a Model 1909 gray green (*grigioverde*) wool vest for infantry troops.

Officer's Model 1909 gray green (*grigioverde*) "cordellino" fabric tunic from a 2nd lieutenant serving in St.Etienne machinegun company.

1st lieutenat's Model 1909 gray green (*grigioverde*) "cordellino" fabric tunic for Alpini troops.

Flag from an *Alpini Squadriglia Automitragliatrici* (Armored car unit for Alpine troops) armed with Model 1909 St. Etienne machineguns.

Unit insignia patches from: Machine gunners Villa Perosa Model 1915 *(pistola mitragliatrice),* Machine gunners Fiat Model 1914, Machine gunners St. Etienne Model 1907, 884th Machine gunners company, Arditi (officer), Militari Arditi, Ski, *Lanciabombe* (bomb throwers) Bettica e Thevenot, Trench mortars/artillery, Sappers, Scouts, Cyclist, and Hand grenade throwers.

Model 1914 Leather belt with iron buckle for NCOs.

Model 1914 Leather belt with brass buckle for officers.

Late war vintage puttees made from gray green (*grigioverde*) ersatz material.

Matching pair of five pointed star collar insignia with screw-back fasteners (*Stellette*).

Forward and reverse views of a Great War commemorative medal and ribbon1915-1918 (*Medaglia commemorativa Guerra* 1915-1918).

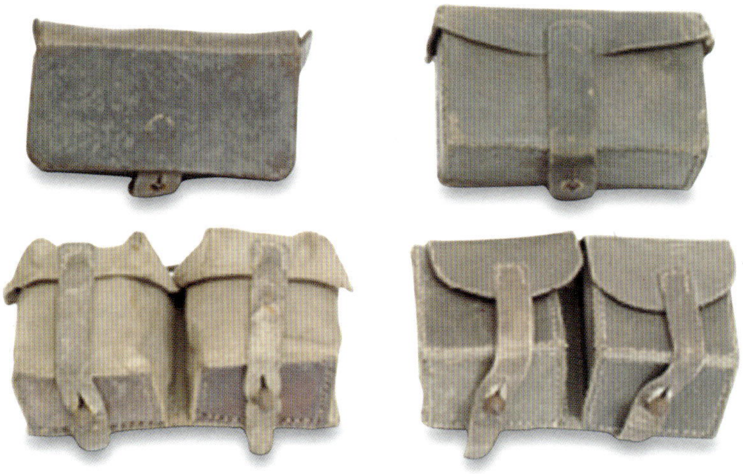

Forward and reverse views of ammo pouches.

Model 1907 canvas bread bag with metal and leather fittings.

Dispatch pouch for messengers/clerks.

Forward and reverse views of a medical carrying case with leather and canvas straps.

Period medical bandage.

Model 1907 backpack for infantry troops. The cloth backpack with leather straps consists of a main compartment divided by cloth and three external center and side pockets.

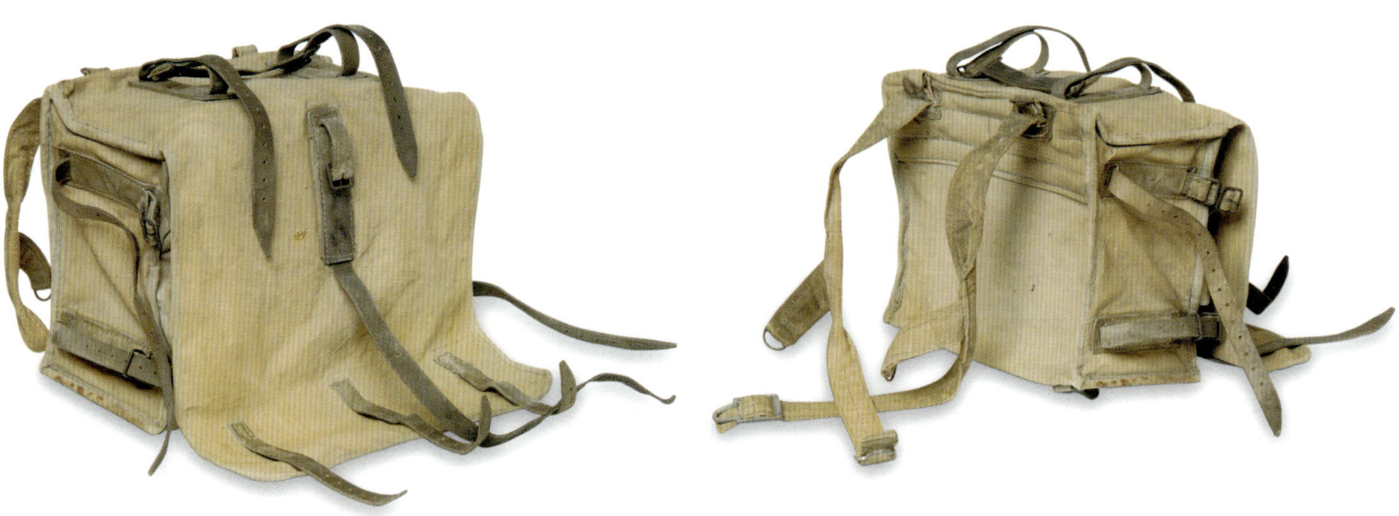

Model 1909 backpack for Alpine troops (*Alpini*).

Mid to late war infantry backpack based the Model 1907. These backpacks are made of ersatz material and have no leather and very few metal fittings.

Medical canteen with wool cover and leather straps. Stretcher-bearers used these canteens.

Bottom: Left: Model 1907 wood (poplar or willow) canteen with canvas strap and screw-in wood plug/stopper. Center: Model 1917 metal canteen with gray green (*grigioverde*) wool cover and canvas strap. Right: Model 1917 metal canteen with gray green (*grigioverde*) wool cover and canvas strap.

Forward and reverse views of a Model 1896 mess kit (*gavetta*).

Depot issued Model 1896 drinking cup.

Different models of food heaters issued to Italian troops. These were recovered from the Adamello glacier.

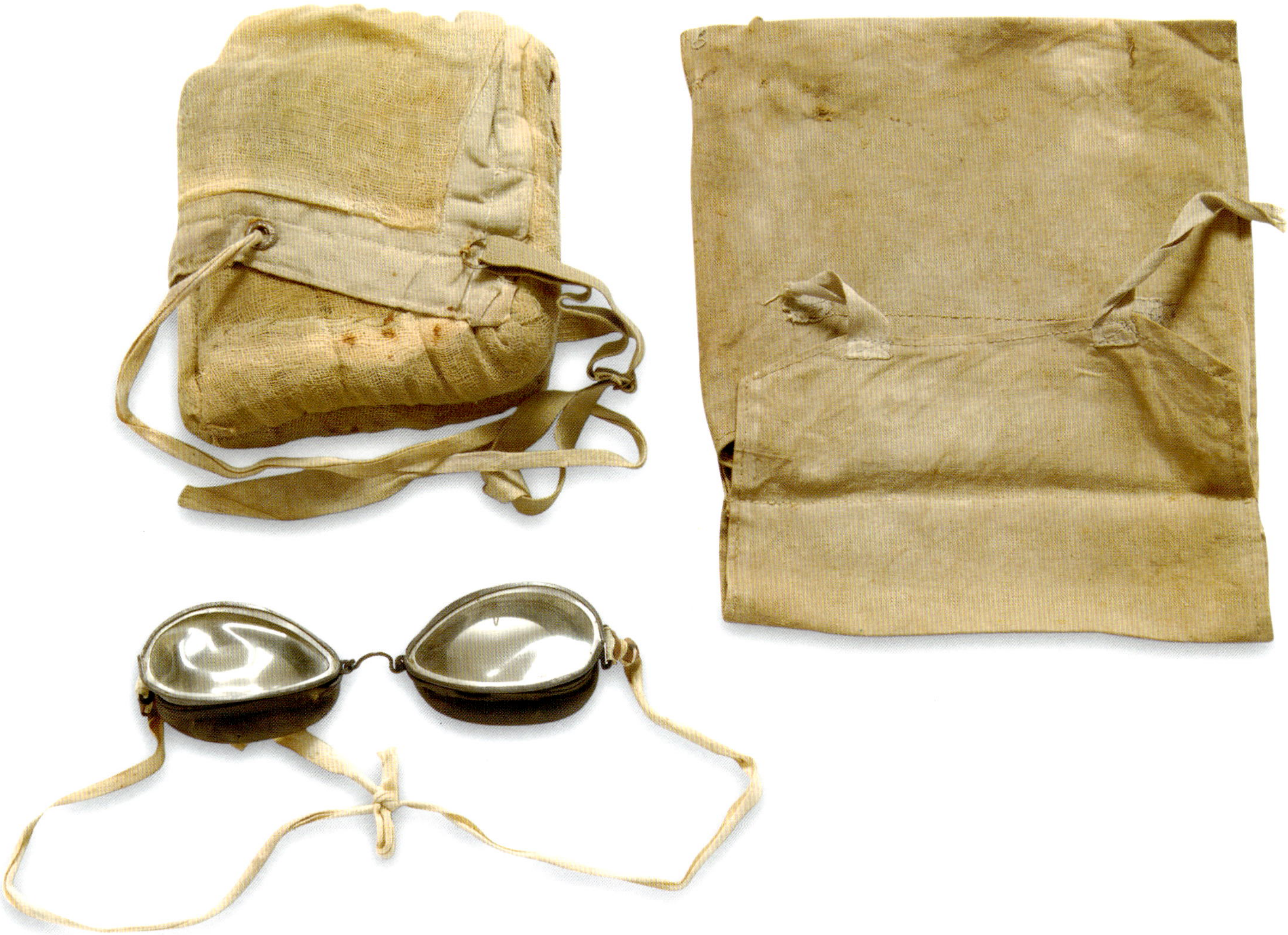

Separate protection *Polivalente* Model 1916 gasmask.

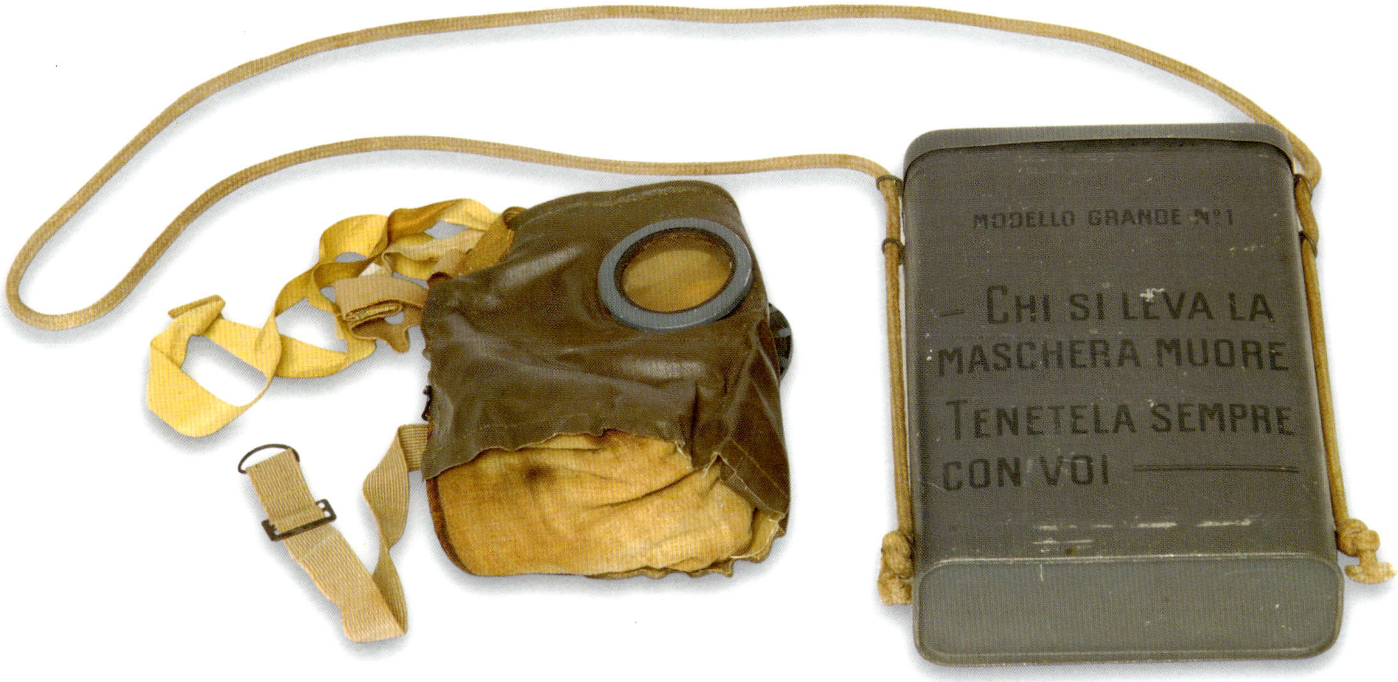

French M2 gasmask for Italian troops stamped 1917.

Polivalente gasmask with metal canister.

British manufactured anti-gas respirator with SBR (Small Box Respirator). These were issued to Italian troops in 1918 after the battle of Caporetto because the *Polivalente* proved ineffective against Blue Cross gas.

Glacier goggles. Such goggles were also used for protection against shrapnel splinters. Note the metal lenses on the pair recovered from a battlefield show damage from the inside out.

Top S.I.P.E (*Societ· Italiana Prodotti Esplosivi*)grenade converted into trench art. Tonalewacht 1916.

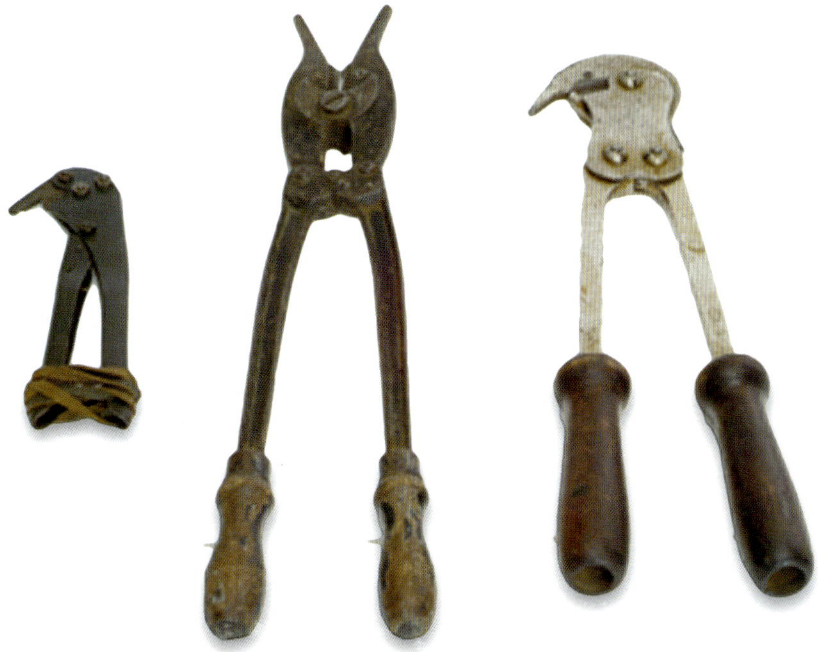

Three models of wire cutters used by the Italian Armed forces.

Late to post war period *Arditi* lapel pin.

Arsenal stamped Model 1891 bayonet with leather scabbard.

Steel protection plate for a Model 1891 Carcano bolt-action rifle. Such protection plates were preferred and often issued to snipers.

Three models of *Arditi* daggers: 1) 1st Model with a blade from a Model 1870/87 Vetterli bayonet 2) Variation of the 1st Model with a blade from a Model 1891 bayonet 3) 2nd Model with a blade from a 1870/87 Vetterli bayonet.

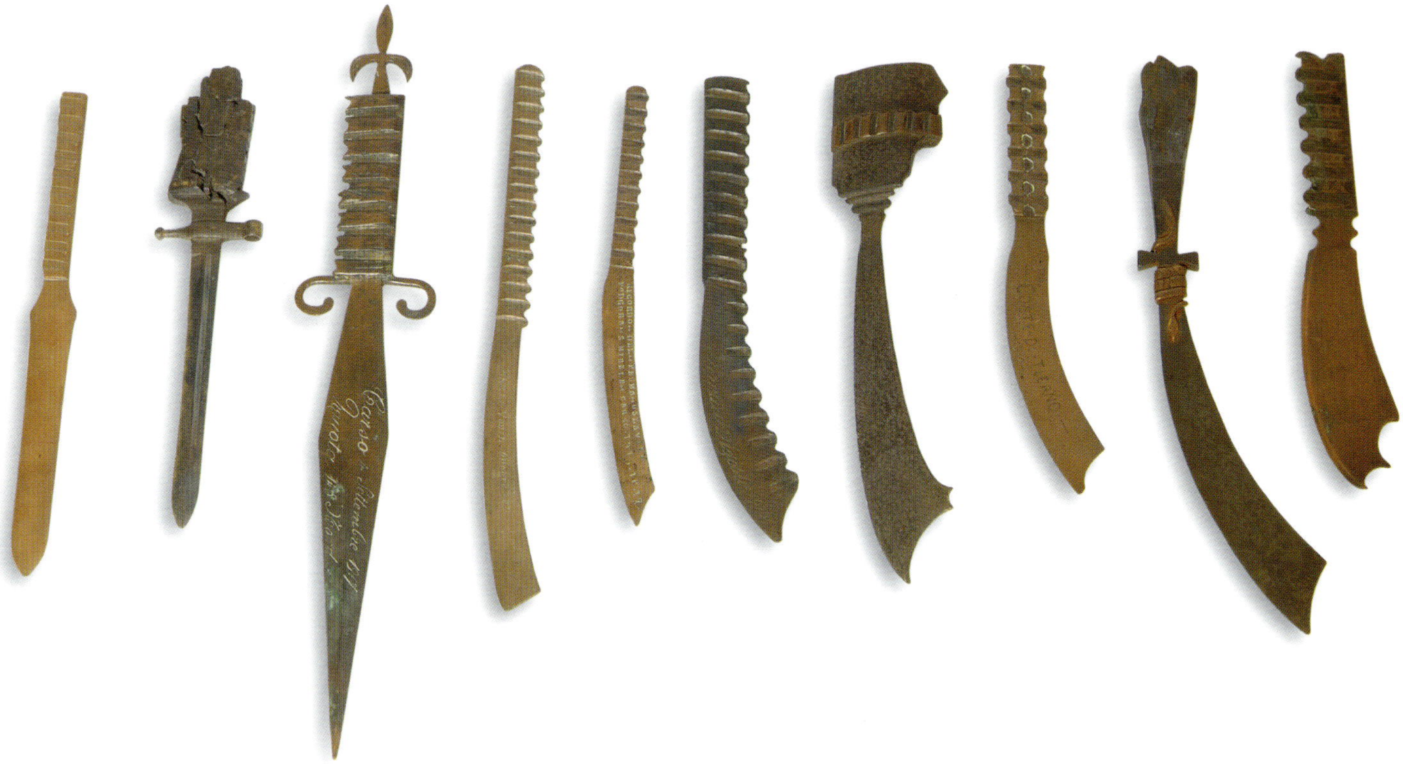

Trench art letter openers made from grenade parts and pieces.

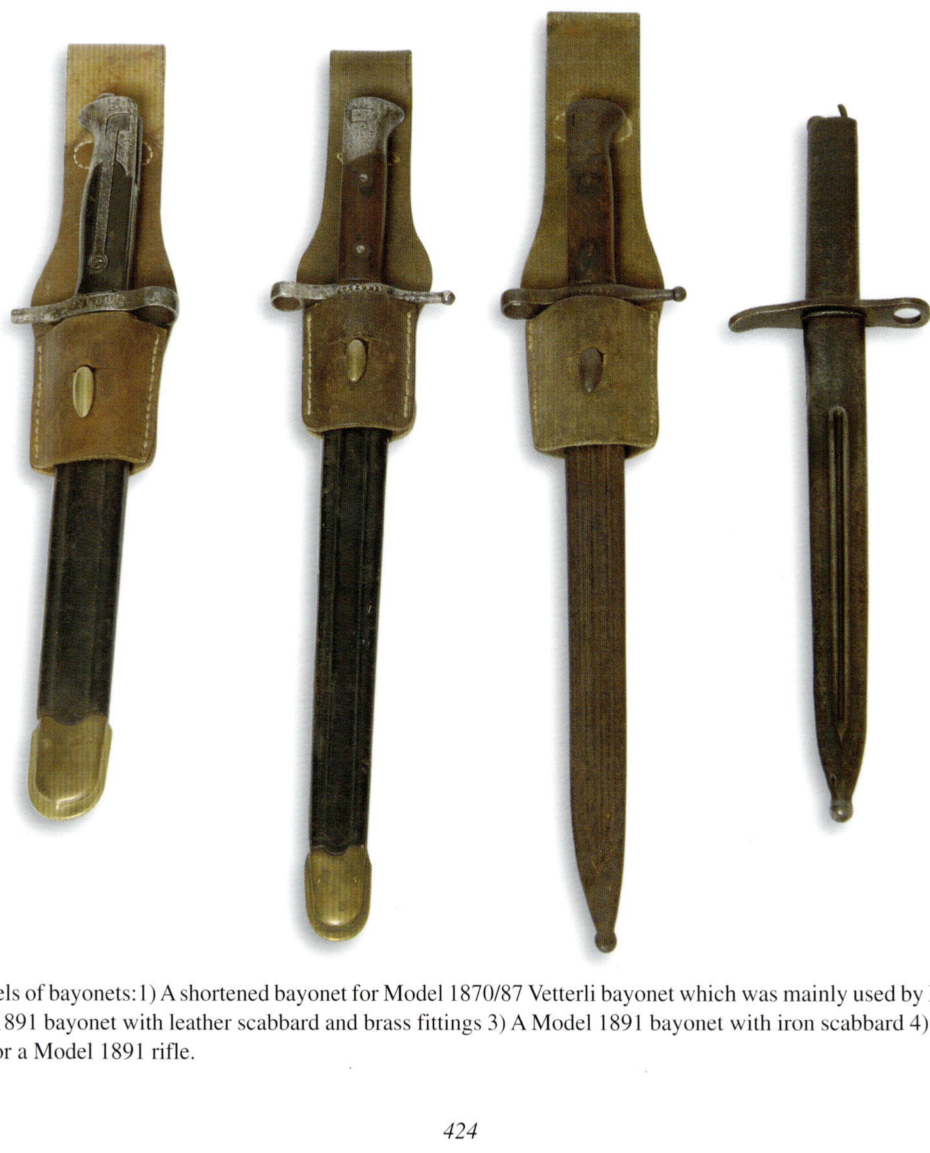

Four models of bayonets:1) A shortened bayonet for Model 1870/87 Vetterli bayonet which was mainly used by Militia. 2) A Model 1891 bayonet with leather scabbard and brass fittings 3) A Model 1891 bayonet with iron scabbard 4) An ersatz bayonet for a Model 1891 rifle.

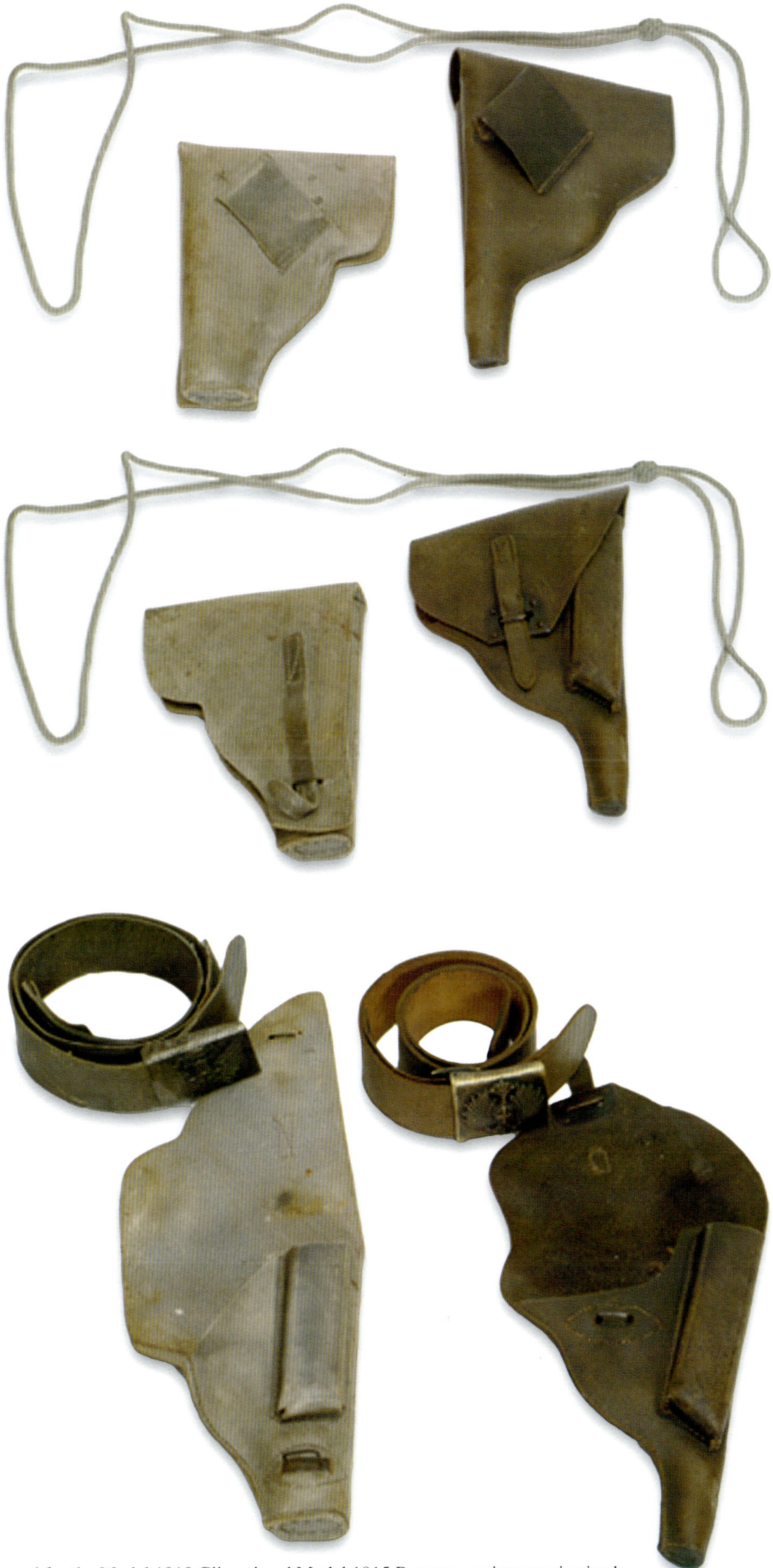

Leather holsters and a lanyard for the Model 1910 Glisenti and Model 1915 Berretta semiautomatic pistols.

Rifle support mount.

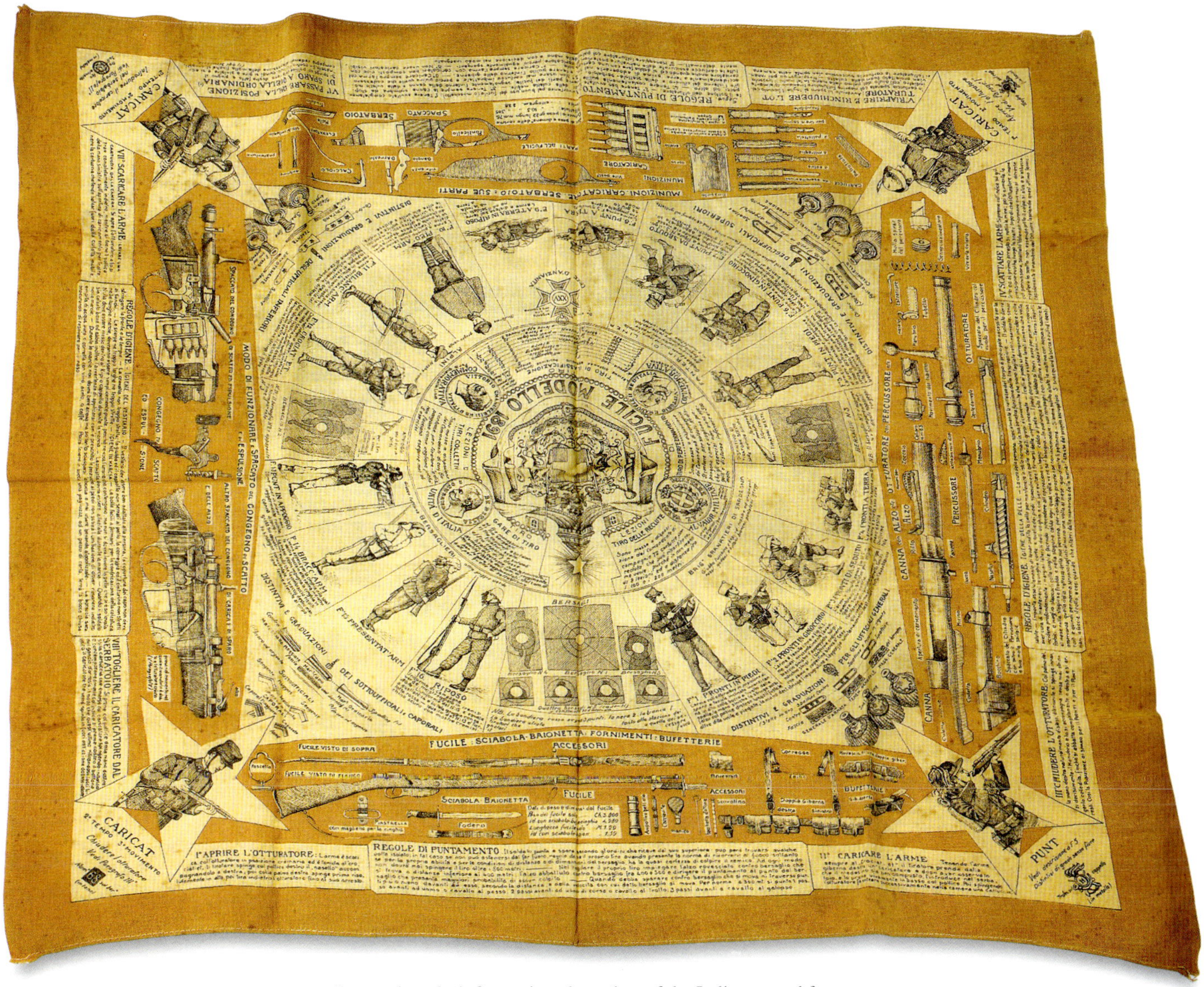

Instruction cloth for various branches of the Italian armed forces.

Chart of collar insignia from 1914.

Appendix

A study conducted during the spring and winter of 1915 concerned identifying a soldier's unit by observing the letters and numbers on his shoulder boards/straps (*Spalline*). The study concluded that while their were many consistencies in numbering and lettering systems appearing on a soldier's *Spalline* there were even more inconsistencies thus, although there were regulations existing however, not rigidly, if at all enforced. *That's Italian!*

Aerostieri (Air Service): Letters ***Ar***
Alpini: Company (*Compagnia*) number
Artillery (field, heavy, horse and train): Company (*Compagnia*) number if train otherwise, battery number.
Artillery (mountain): Battery number
Artillery (fortress): Company (*Compagnia*) number
***Bersaglieri*:** Battalion (*Battaglione*) number
Bersaglieri ciclisti* (bicyclists):** Letter ***C and Battalion (*Battaglione*) number
Bersaglieri ciclisti* machinegunners:** Letter ***M, battalion (*Battaglione*) number and letter ***C***.
Bersaglieri* machinegunners:** Letter ***M and Battalion (*Battaglione*) number
***Cavalleria* (Cavalry):** Squadron (*Squadriglia*) number
Cavalleria* machinegun units:** Letter ***M
Deposito* (Depot /Quartermaster):** Letter ***D
Dirigibilisti Battaglione (Dirigible Battalion): Letters ***Dr***
***Fanteria* (Infantry):** Company (*Compagnia*) number
***Fanteria* (Infantry)**
Mitragliatrici (Machinegunners): Number and letter ***M***
***Genio*(Engineers):** Company (*Compagnia*) number
Lanciafiamme* (Flamethrower):** Section number and letters ***LF
Milizia mobile* (Mobile Militia):** Letters ***MM
Milizia Territoriale* (Home guard/Territorial Militia):** Letters ***MT
Parco Automobilisti* (Vehicle Parkers/Drivers):** Letters ***PA
Regia Marina (Naval/Marine Landing Party): Company (*Compagnia*) number
***Sanita* (Medical units):** Company (*Compagnia*) number
Scoule aviatori (Aviator/Pilot/Flight School/Academy): Letters ***SC***
Specialisti aviazione di artiglieria (Air Service Artillery Specialist): Letters ***Sp. A***
Squadriglie aviatori (Aviator/Pilot Squadron): Letters ***SQ***
Squadriglie aviazione per artiglieria (Air Squadrons for Artillery): Letters ***Av. A***
Stato Maggiore (General Staff /Headquarters): Letters ***SM***

Glossary

Uniforms, Headdresses, and Equipment
Badiletto: shovel
Berretto: field cap
Berretti: field caps (plural)
Borraccia: canteen
Bustina: forage cap/ side cap/tent hat with visor
Bustine: plural of *bustina*
Cappello: *Alpini* field cap
Cinturone: belt
Colbacco: cylindrically shaped headdress made of fur or felt
Cupolino: dome shaped Model 1915 field cap
Elmo/elmetto: helmet
Fasce mollettiere: leggings /puttees
Fibbia: buckle
Fregio: badge
Gambali: leather gaiters
Gavetta: mess kit
Giacca: tunic
Giberna: ammo pouch
Lancieri: Lancers
Lanterna: trench lantern
Lucerna: *Carabinieri* headdress
Mantellina: cloak
Medaglia: medal
Moretto: *Bersaglieri* headdress
Mostrine/i: cloth collar patches
Nastrino: ribbon
Occhiali: goggles
Pantaloni: pants, trousers
Puimetto: plumes of a *Bersaglieri Moretto*
Piccozzino: pick used for entrenching or climbing
Ramponi: iron cleats used for climbing
Scarpe: field shoes/ankle boots
Scodellino: dome shaped Model 1915 field cap
Scudo: trench shield
Soldato: soldier
Soldati: soldiers (plural)
Spallacci: suspenders
Spalline: shoulder straps
Speroni: spurs
Stellette: five pointed star collar insignia
Stivali: boots
Tascapane: bread bag
Telino: a cloth cover for a helmet
Vanghetta: shovel
Zaino: backpack

Weaponry
Armatura: body armor
Baionetta: bayonet
Bomba a mano: hand grenade
Bomba da fucile: rifle grenade
Bombarda: trench mortar
Corazza: body armor
Dragona: bayonet frog
Fodero: scabbard
Fondina: holster
Fucile: rifle
Lanciafiamme: flamethrower
Mazza: mace or trench club
Mitragliatrice: machinegun
Moschetto: rifle
Pistola: pistol
Pugnale: dagger
Sciabola: saber
Spada: sword

Branches of the Armed Forces
Alpini: Alpinists or Alpine Troops. Nicknamed "penne nere" or "black feathers".
Arditi: Fearless, bold, audacious assault troops
Artiglieria: Artillery
Artiglieria a cavallo: Horse drawn or mounted artillery
Artiglieria da fortezza: Fortress artillery
Artiglieria da montagna: Mountain artillery (Used in Alpini units)
Artiglieria pesante Heavy Field Artillery
campale/ da compagna:
Artillery su treno: Train or Railway Artillery
Bersaglieri: Elite/Guard troops. Famous for wearing plumes in their headgear.
Bersaglieri ciclisti: Elite/Guard troop bicyclists. Bicycle unit.
Cavaleria: Cavalry
Corpo Aeronautico: Air Corps
Fanteria: Infantry
Genio: Engineers
Genio minatori: Excavation engineers (Digging trenches etc.)
Genio pontieri: Bridge building engineers
Genio transmissioni: Transmission engineers
Genio zappatori: Sappers
Granatieri: Grenadiers
Milizia mobile: Mobil militia
Milizia territoriale: Territorial Militia or Home guard
Sanit·: Medical units
Sciatori/Skiatori: Ski troops/units
Stato Maggiore: General Staff / General Headquarters
Sussistenza: Supply units
Trasporti: Transport units

Units
Battaglione: Battalion
Compagnia: Company
Corpo d'Armata: Army Corps

Divisione: Division
Plotone: Platoon
Reggimento di Fanteria: Infantry Regiment
Reggimento di Cavalleria: Cavalry Regiment
Squadriglia: Squadron

Ranks (Rough Equivalents)
Appuntato: Private First Class
Caporale: Corporal
Caporale Maggiore: Lance Corporal
Capitano: Captain
Fante: Enlisted rank soldier
Maresciallo: Warrant officer
Sergente: Sergeant
Sergente Maggiore: Sergeant Major
Ufficiale: Officer
Volontario: Volunteer

Transport
Aereo: airplane
Aeroplano: airplane
Aerostato: observation balloon/blimp
Automobile: car
Bicicletta: bicycle
Dirigibile: airship/zeppelin
Camion: truck
Carro: cart
Carro Armato: tank
Cavallo: horse
Mulo: mules (widely used by *Alpini*)

Expressions and Terms
Tiratore scelto: sniper
Cecchino: Nickname for Austro-Hungarian snipers (*Scharfschütze*). As the war progressed, *Cecchino* was the nickname used for Italian snipers as well.
Francesco: Nickname for snipers. Derived from the Italian translation of the Austro-Hungarian Emperor's name Franz Josef; *Francesco Guiseppe.*
Ghirba: Archaic word for canteen.
Salvare la ghirba!: "Save the canteen" meaning "returning alive"
Grigioverde: Gray green.
Vestire il grigioverde!: "to wear the gray green!" meaning "to enter the army!"
Me ne frego!: "I could not give a damn!" an *Arditi* expression

Further Reading

Die Italienische Armee;1913 Vienna, Austria 1913.

Die Italienische Armee;1917 Berlin, Germany 1917.

Armi ed Equipaggiamenti dell'esercito Italiano nella Grande Guerra 1915-1918. Nevio Mantoan. Gino Rossato Editore. Via Bella Venezia 1996.

The Guns of August. Barbara Tuchmann. Dell Publishing Co., Inc. New York, New York 1963.

Great Battles of World War I. Anthony Livesey. Macmillan Publishing Company. New York, New York 1989.